GENERATIVE AI MASTERY

A Strategic Roadmap for Business Transformation

Ethan Westwood

SMART B O O K S

"Generative AI represents a revolutionary leap in technology, offering businesses the ability to innovate, optimize processes, and create transformative experiences by harnessing the power of intelligent automation and creative problem-solving."

Ethan Westwood

Table of Contents

Introduction: The Generative AI Revolution **15**

Purpose of This Book.. 16

Why Executives Need a Clear AI Strategy 18

The Transformative Potential of Generative AI 19

Chapter 1: Demystifying Generative AI........................ **23**

1.1 What Is Generative AI? 23

1.1.1 Key Outputs of Generative AI:........................... 24

1.2 Key Capabilities and Technological Foundations...... 27

1.2.1 Neural Networks: 27

1.2.2 Large Language Models (LLMs):........................ 29

1.2.3 Reinforcement Learning:................................... 31

1.2.4 Multi-Modal Integration: 32

1.3 Strengths and Limitations of Generative AI 34

1.3.1 Strengths of Generative AI:............................... 35

1.3.2 Limitations of Generative AI: 37

1.4 Real-World Examples of Business Impact 40

1.4.1 E-commerce Personalization 40

1.4.2 Product Design... 41

1.4.3 Customer Support 42

1.4.4 Expanding the Business Strategy Framework with Generative AI 44

Chapter 2: Strategic Alignment—Mapping AI to Business Objectives 46

2.1 Identifying High-Impact Use Cases 46

2.1.1 Stakeholder Interviews 46

2.1.2 Data Inventory 47

2.1.3 Customer-Centric Design 48

2.1.4 Example Framework for Identifying AI Opportunities 49

2.1.5 Refining the Use Case Selection: 51

2.2 Aligning AI Initiatives with Core Strategies 52

2.2.1 Defining Success Metrics................................... 53

2.2.2 Cross-Functional Collaboration 55

2.2.3 Aligning AI with Business Goals 57

2.2.4 Establishing a Governance Framework.............. 58

2.2.5 Measuring and Refining AI Impact 59

2.3 Prioritization Frameworks....................................... 60

2.3.1 Impact Potential... 61

2.3.2 Feasibility.. 62

2.3.3 Risk Level.. 64

2.3.4 Example Scoring System: 66

2.4 Risk Assessment and Mitigation Strategies 68

2.4.1 Bias Audits 69

2.4.2 Human Oversight 70

2.4.3 Regulatory Compliance 72

2.4.4 Transparency and Explainability 73

2.4.5 Intellectual Property (IP) Protection 74

Chapter 3: Talent and Capability Development............ 76

3.1 Building an AI-Ready Workforce............................. 77

3.1.1 Leadership Training in AI Fundamentals 77

3.1.2 Cross-Departmental Skill Development 79

3.1.3 Structured Learning Paths............................... 80

3.1.4 Creating Organizational AI Fluency 81

3.2 Upskilling Existing Teams 83

3.2.1 Data Literacy as a Foundation 84

3.2.2 Specialized AI Training 85

3.2.3 Hands-On Learning with AI Tools...................... 87

3.2.4 Mentorship Programs 88

3.3 Attracting and Retaining AI Talent 89

3.3.1 Building a Strong Employer Brand in AI 90

3.3.2 Competitive Compensation and Benefits 91

3.3.3 Creating a Dynamic, Inclusive Workplace 92

3.3.4 Opportunities for Career Development.............. 93

3.4 Creating a Culture of Innovation and Continuous
Learning 94

3.4.1 Encourage Experimentation and Risk-Taking 95

3.4.2 Fostering Collaboration Across Departments 96

3.4.3 Promote Knowledge Sharing 97

3.4.4 Embedding AI in Organizational Strategy 98

Chapter 4: Technology Integration and Infrastructure . 100

4.1 Assessing Current IT Capabilities 103

4.1.1 Evaluating Data Infrastructure 104

4.1.2 Evaluating Computational Power and Cloud
Readiness 106

4.1.3 Assessing System Interoperability 107

4.2 Make vs. Buy Decision Frameworks 109

4.2.1 Build (Make): Custom AI Solutions 110

4.2.2 Buy (Buy): Pre-Built AI Solutions 112

4.2.3 Hybrid Approach: Combining Make and Buy 114

4.3 Selecting the Right AI Technologies and Partners ... 117

4.3.1 Evaluating AI Technologies............................. 118

4.3.2 Choosing AI Partners 120

4.3.3 Vendor Evaluation Criteria 122

4.3.4 Strategic Considerations for Partnering in AI 124

4.4 Ensuring Scalability and Compatibility 125

4.4.1 Cloud-Based Solutions for Scalability 125

4.4.2 Modular Architecture 127

4.4.3 Ensuring Integration with Legacy Systems 128

Chapter 5: Implementation and Scaling Strategies 131

5.1 Pilot Program Design 132

5.1.1 Defining the Pilot Scope and Objectives 133

5.1.2 Choosing the Right Use Cases for Pilot Testing 134

5.1.3 Stakeholder Engagement and Communication 136

5.2 Metrics-Driven Expansion 137

5.2.1 Key Performance Indicators (KPIs) for Scaling AI
.... 138

5.2.2 Data-Driven Decision Making 140

5.2.3 Scaling Based on Success 141

5.3 Best Practices for Successful Rollout 143

5.3.1 Start Small, Scale Gradually. 143

5.3.2 Cross-Functional Collaboration 144

5.3.3 Continuous Monitoring and Feedback 146

5.4 Case Studies of Effective Implementation.............. 148

5.4.1 Case Study: AI in Customer Service at a Telecom Provider.. 148

5.4.2 Case Study: AI-Powered Content Creation in Marketing 150

5.4.3 Case Study: AI in Healthcare Diagnostics 151

Chapter 6: Ethical Governance and Risk Management 154

6.1 Addressing AI Bias and Reliability Concerns........... 155

6.1.1 Identifying and Mitigating Bias 155

6.1.2 Reliability and Accountability in AI Systems 158

6.2 Data Privacy and Security Protocols 161

6.2.1 Ensuring Compliance with Data Privacy Laws .. 162

6.2.2 Implementing Strong Data Security Measures . 164

6.2.3 Data Privacy and Security in AI Governance 167

6.3 Developing Responsible AI Frameworks 168

6.3.1 Establishing Ethical AI Guidelines 169

6.3.2 Creating an AI Ethics Board or Governance Committee 171

6.3.3 Fostering a Culture of Responsibility in AI 174

6.4 Compliance and Regulatory Considerations 175

6.4.1 Understanding the Global Regulatory Landscape 175

6.4.2 Preparing for Audits and Regulatory Scrutiny ... 178

Chapter 7: Organizational Change Management 183

7.1 Securing Leadership Commitment 184

7.1.1 Defining a Clear Vision for AI 184

7.1.2 Establishing a Governance Structure............... 185

7.1.3 Allocating Resources for AI Initiatives 187

7.1.4 Measuring and Communicating Progress 189

7.2 Change Communication Strategies 190

7.2.1 Building a Transparent Communication Plan ... 191

7.2.2 Tailored Messaging for Different Stakeholders . 192

7.2.3 Managing Expectations 194

7.3 Workforce Preparation and Adoption 195

7.3.1 Upskilling and Reskilling Programs 196

7.3.2 Developing a Knowledge Sharing Culture......... 198

7.3.3 Job Redesign and AI Augmentation 199

7.3.4 Fostering Employee Buy-In Through Training and Involvement... 201

7.4 Overcoming Resistance and Building AI Literacy 202

7.4.1 Addressing Fear of Job Displacement 202

7.4.2 Building AI Literacy Across the Organization 204

7.4.3 Promoting a Growth Mindset 205

Chapter 8: Measuring and Optimizing AI Value 208

8.1 Key Performance Indicators (KPIs) 209

8.2 Feedback Loops and Continuous Improvement 212

8.3 Quantifying AI's Business Impact 216

8.3.1 Calculating ROI (Return on Investment) 217

8.3.2 Business Impact of AI on Key Drivers 219

8.3.3 Attribution Modeling 221

8.3.4 Long-Term Value Creation 221

8.4 Adaptive Strategy Development 222

8.4.1 Embracing a Test-and-Learn Approach 223

8.4.2 Strategic Flexibility in AI Use Cases 224

8.4.3 Continuous Reassessment of Business Needs 225

8.4.4 Agility in Decision-Making 226

Chapter 9: Future-Proofing Your AI Strategy 228

9.1 Emerging AI Trends 228

9.2 Investment in R&D 232

9.3 Building Organizational Agility 234

9.4 Preparing for Rapid Technological Evolution 236

Glossary of AI Terms.. **239**

Assessment Tools and Frameworks........................... **243**

    AI Maturity Model 243

    AI Use Case Evaluation Framework 253

    AI Readiness Assessment 262

    AI Risk Management Framework 271

Final Chapter: Towards a Future Powered by Generative AI **281**

Introduction: The Generative AI Revolution

Generative Artificial Intelligence (AI) represents a groundbreaking technological leap that rivals, if not surpasses, the transformative power of the Internet and mobile computing. Historically, AI has been used primarily for tasks such as data analysis, pattern recognition, and automation, helping businesses optimize operations and gain insights from vast amounts of data.

However, generative AI takes this a step further by introducing the capacity to create—content, designs, models, strategies, and even entirely new solutions to complex problems. Unlike traditional AI, which simply analyzes existing data, generative AI can generate novel outputs that were previously thought to require human creativity or expertise.

For business leaders, this shift represents more than just an incremental evolution in technology; it marks the arrival of an entirely new paradigm that fundamentally alters the landscape of innovation, productivity, and competition. The ability to rapidly prototype ideas, design unique products, or craft tailored marketing strategies with the help of generative AI opens up unprecedented opportunities for organizations.

Companies can now leverage AI to scale creativity, reduce costs, and enhance decision-making processes. In a competitive business environment, those who harness the potential of generative AI will be better positioned to innovate faster, improve operational efficiency, and ultimately maintain a competitive edge in their respective industries. This transformative shift will reshape industries, redefine value chains, and catalyze a new era of innovation across sectors such as healthcare, entertainment, manufacturing, and beyond.

Generative AI Benefits

| Develop New Products | Customer Support | Improve Task Efficiency | Boost Personalization | Data Analysis & Insights | Language Translation & Communication |

Purpose of This Book

This book serves as a comprehensive and practical guide specifically designed for senior executives who are looking to navigate the rapidly evolving landscape of generative AI. It offers deep, actionable insights into how to leverage this powerful technology strategically to drive meaningful business transformation. In today's fast-paced and highly competitive business environment, understanding how to effectively integrate generative AI is not just an option—it's a necessity for staying ahead of the curve.

Whether you're a CEO focused on mapping your organization's future growth, a Chief Technology Officer (CTO) exploring next-generation technological solutions, or a strategy consultant advising clients on how to adapt to emerging trends, this book provides tailored, actionable strategies that will help you harness the full potential of generative AI.

The content is designed to bridge the gap between theoretical AI concepts and practical business applications, ensuring that you can translate advanced AI capabilities into tangible results for your organization.

The book delves into key areas such as developing AI-driven business models, improving operational efficiency through automation, fostering innovation, and navigating the challenges that come with implementing such transformative technologies. With case studies, expert advice, and step-by-step guidance, it empowers decision-makers to make informed choices about how to integrate generative AI into their organization's processes, products, and services.

By following the strategies outlined in this book, business leaders can ensure that their organizations not only survive but thrive in the age of AI, positioning themselves as pioneers and leaders in their respective industries.

Whether you're in the early stages of AI adoption or already experimenting with its capabilities, this book serves as a valuable resource to help you stay at the forefront of the AI revolution and successfully lead your organization through this technological transformation.

Why Executives Need a Clear AI Strategy

AI is no longer a luxury or "nice-to-have" technology for organizations—it has become a critical "must-have" for staying competitive and relevant in an increasingly technology-driven world. For today's executives, this reality presents a dual challenge: not only must they keep pace with the rapid advancements in AI technology, but they must also ensure that AI initiatives are deeply aligned with their organization's core mission and long-term strategic goals. The stakes are high, as adopting AI improperly or in a disjointed manner can lead to inefficiencies or missed opportunities. At the same time, the potential for transformative impact is immense, and executives must carefully navigate this landscape to ensure that AI investments deliver measurable value to the business and its stakeholders.

Generative AI stands at the forefront of this technological evolution, offering unprecedented capabilities to create innovative solutions across various industries. However, the power of generative AI comes with significant complexity. Its ability to generate content, design, models, and strategies opens up new avenues for creativity and productivity, but it also introduces challenges related to ethical concerns, data privacy, and integration with existing systems.

The adoption of generative AI must, therefore, be approached with caution, requiring a well-thought-out strategy that not only mitigates risks but also maximizes its potential for long-term success. Leaders must ensure that AI is introduced thoughtfully, with a clear understanding of its implications and a roadmap for sustainable implementation.

The Transformative Potential of Generative AI

Generative AI is already reshaping industries, driving innovation, and creating opportunities for businesses to achieve competitive advantages that were previously unimaginable. Its potential to revolutionize key sectors is evident across multiple domains:

Healthcare: In healthcare, generative AI is making significant strides by enabling the generation of personalized treatment plans tailored to individual patients. AI-driven models can simulate drug molecules, identify potential therapeutic compounds, and predict patient outcomes, drastically accelerating the process of medical research and development. This not only shortens the time to market for new drugs and therapies but also improves the accuracy of diagnoses and treatment efficacy, ultimately improving patient outcomes and reducing healthcare costs.

Finance: In the finance sector, generative AI is transforming investment strategies and portfolio management. AI models can generate personalized investment plans based on an individual's financial goals, risk appetite, and market conditions. Furthermore, by using predictive analytics, AI can analyze vast amounts of data to forecast market trends, detect anomalies, and suggest real-time adjustments to investment strategies. This allows financial institutions to make more informed, data-driven decisions, improving their ability to manage risk, optimize returns, and offer more personalized services to clients.

Media and Entertainment: The media and entertainment industries are leveraging generative AI to automate content creation and design, resulting in significant cost reductions while maintaining creative quality. AI tools are being used to generate everything from music and video content to marketing materials and digital artwork. This not only empowers creatives by streamlining tedious tasks but also allows for rapid experimentation with new ideas and content formats. Additionally, AI-driven tools are being employed to generate scripts, video sequences, and even interactive experiences, expanding the possibilities for storytelling and audience engagement.

Manufacturing: In manufacturing, generative AI is revolutionizing product development by optimizing design processes through AI-powered generative design. By using advanced algorithms, AI can create innovative, highly efficient product designs that would be difficult or impossible for humans to conceive. This reduces material waste, lowers production costs, and improves overall product performance. Additionally, AI can simulate manufacturing processes to predict potential issues before they arise, enabling companies to fine-tune production methods and streamline supply chains, ultimately leading to higher productivity and cost savings.

The Transformative Potential of Generative AI

Healthcare Finance Media & Entertainment Manufacturing

As generative AI continues to evolve, its potential to reshape industries will only grow, creating new avenues for growth, innovation, and operational efficiency. For executives, the key challenge lies in understanding how to harness this technology in a way that aligns with their organization's vision and long-term strategy, while managing the risks and complexities that come with it. This requires careful planning, thoughtful integration, and continuous adaptation to ensure that the transformative power of generative AI is fully realized.

The impact of generative AI is vast, but the key to leveraging it lies in strategic, disciplined execution—precisely the focus of this book.

Chapter 1: Demystifying Generative AI

1.1 What Is Generative AI?

At its core, generative AI refers to a category of algorithms designed to create new content, ideas, or solutions based on input data. Unlike traditional AI systems that primarily focus on tasks such as classification, pattern recognition, or analysis, generative AI goes a step further by producing original and often highly creative outputs. These systems leverage advanced machine learning techniques, particularly deep learning, to learn patterns and structures from large datasets and then use this knowledge to generate novel content or solve problems. This ability to produce original results makes generative AI uniquely powerful, as it opens up new possibilities for automation, innovation, and efficiency across various fields.

One of the key distinctions of generative AI is that it does not merely process or evaluate data—it generates something entirely new that closely resembles or extends the input data. For instance, where traditional AI systems might classify an image as a "cat," generative AI could generate a new, realistic image of a cat from scratch, combining learned attributes and features. This capacity for creating new content across different formats is transforming industries and revolutionizing workflows by making processes more efficient and enabling creative possibilities that were previously limited by human capability or computational resources.

1.1.1 Key Outputs of Generative AI:

1. **Text**: One of the most widely recognized applications of generative AI is in natural language processing, where AI models generate human-like text. These models can write articles, generate code, produce responses in natural language, or even create entire books. Whether it's generating customer support responses, drafting legal documents, or writing creative content such as stories and poetry, generative AI has the power to replicate and even enhance human-like writing. Its ability to generate contextually relevant and coherent text makes it an invaluable tool for content creation across a wide array of industries.

2. **Images**: Generative AI is also revolutionizing visual content creation. AI models can generate images that range from artistic designs and illustrations to highly

detailed, realistic renderings. By understanding and synthesizing patterns from vast image datasets, these models can create original images based on a prompt, whether that's producing product designs, generating visual content for advertisements, or creating entirely new artwork. In industries like fashion, graphic design, and entertainment, generative AI is enabling faster, more cost-effective creative workflows and opening up new avenues for artistic expression.

3. **Audio**: In the realm of audio, generative AI can compose music, generate sound effects, or even create human-like voices. AI models are capable of learning the structure of different genres of music or speech patterns to generate original compositions or simulate voices that mimic real human speech. These capabilities are being leveraged in various applications, from creating personalized soundtracks for movies and video games to enhancing virtual assistants with more natural-sounding voices. The ability to generate realistic and contextually appropriate audio content has wide-ranging implications in entertainment, customer service, and more.

4. **Structured Data**: Beyond creative content, generative AI is also making significant strides in generating structured data. This can include creating predictive models, optimizing workflows, or even designing algorithms that improve efficiency and decision-making. For example, in business intelligence, generative AI can synthesize large datasets to predict market trends, optimize inventory systems, or design new business processes. It can also generate code that automates tasks or enhances software development processes, making it a valuable tool for developers and data scientists working to streamline complex operations or create highly tailored solutions.

Generative AI's ability to produce original, valuable outputs across text, images, audio, and structured data fundamentally shifts how organizations and individuals approach creation, innovation, and problem-solving. From enhancing creativity in the arts to optimizing complex business workflows, the potential applications of generative AI are vast and still growing. As these technologies continue to improve and become more accessible, the scope of generative AI's impact on industries will only expand, making it a transformative force across nearly every sector of the economy.

1.2 Key Capabilities and Technological Foundations

Generative AI is built upon several advanced technological pillars that empower it to produce creative, innovative, and often groundbreaking outputs across a variety of domains. These foundational technologies are the driving force behind the rapid evolution and capabilities of generative AI systems. Below are the key components that define and enable the vast potential of generative AI:

1.2.1 Neural Networks:

Neural networks form the bedrock of most generative AI models. These networks mimic the human brain's structure, with layers of interconnected nodes that process and learn from data. Specifically, **Generative Adversarial Networks (GANs), Variational Autoencoders (VAEs)**, and **Transformer models** (like GPT and BERT) are the key architectures that power generative AI:

- **Generative Adversarial Networks (GANs)** consist of two neural networks: a **generator** and a **discriminator**. The generator creates new data (e.g., images, text), while the discriminator evaluates how realistic the generated data is. Over time, the generator improves by trying to fool the discriminator, which pushes both networks to become more sophisticated. This adversarial process enables GANs to produce highly realistic images, video, and other content.

- **Variational Autoencoders (VAEs)** are another class of neural networks used for generating new content. VAEs learn the latent representations of input data and can generate new, similar data by sampling from the learned distribution. VAEs are particularly powerful in tasks like image generation and data compression, as they can capture complex structures in data and reconstruct new, high-quality outputs from them.

- **Transformer Models** like **GPT (Generative Pretrained Transformer)** and **BERT (Bidirectional Encoder Representations from Transformers)** have revolutionized the natural language processing (NLP) field. Transformers use attention mechanisms to process input data in parallel, enabling them to efficiently learn contextual relationships within large datasets. GPT, for instance, is pre-trained on massive amounts of text and then fine-tuned for specific tasks, allowing it to generate coherent, contextually relevant text across diverse domains, from conversational agents to creative writing. BERT, which is more focused on understanding and interpreting text, enables machines to understand the intricacies of language and context, making it invaluable for applications like search engines and language comprehension.

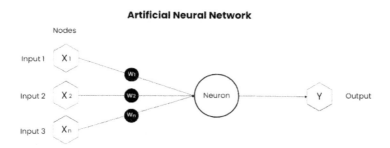

Artificial Neural Network

1.2.2 Large Language Models (LLMs):

Large Language Models (LLMs) such as GPT and BERT are massive neural networks trained on vast corpora of text data from diverse sources. These models have been pre-trained on extensive datasets that include books, articles, websites, and other publicly available written material, allowing them to acquire a broad understanding of human language. Once trained, LLMs can be fine-tuned for specific tasks, such as text generation, sentiment analysis, or question answering. The result is a model that exhibits advanced comprehension, reasoning, and generation capabilities.

These models excel in understanding nuanced language patterns and context, which is crucial for generating realistic, human-like text or interpreting complex language queries. Because of their vast training data and sophisticated architecture, LLMs can produce highly accurate and coherent responses across a wide range of topics, making them powerful tools for businesses seeking to automate customer support, create personalized content, or even generate code. The versatility of LLMs also extends to multilingual capabilities, allowing organizations to create solutions that operate across different languages and regions.

Features of Large Language Models

Transformer-Based Architectures | Hybrid AI Integration | Adaptive AI Capabilities | Responsible AI Practices | Extensive Pre-Training & Fine-Tuning | Tokenization & Embedding Techniques

1.2.3 Reinforcement Learning:

Reinforcement learning (RL) is a type of machine learning where models learn through interaction with their environment. Unlike supervised learning, where the model is trained with labeled data, reinforcement learning involves an agent that takes actions in an environment and receives feedback in the form of rewards or penalties. Over time, the agent learns to optimize its actions to maximize cumulative rewards, improving its performance through trial and error.

In the context of generative AI, reinforcement learning is used to help models refine their outputs by continuously adjusting based on feedback. This iterative learning process allows AI systems to improve their performance over time, making them more effective in tasks such as generating more accurate text, refining designs, or optimizing complex workflows. RL is particularly useful in tasks like game playing, robotics, and autonomous systems, but it also finds

31

applications in generative models where outputs must improve or adapt based on specific goals or criteria.

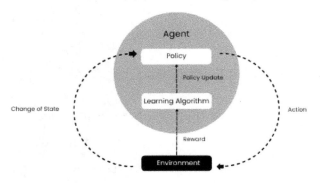

1.2.4 Multi-Modal Integration:

One of the most exciting advancements in generative AI is the ability to integrate multiple types of data—text, images, audio, and other formats—into a single model, a capability known as **multi-modal integration**. This allows generative AI models to process and generate outputs across different modalities simultaneously, creating more immersive and context-aware applications. For instance, a multi-modal AI system might generate an image based on a text description, create audio to accompany the image, or generate an entire video from a narrative script.

This capability enables richer and more interactive AI applications. For example, in creative industries, a generative AI could assist in producing videos that combine script writing, visual effects, and sound design—all tailored to a specific theme or narrative. In healthcare, AI might combine medical text data with visual scans to generate reports or assist in diagnostics. By working across multiple modalities, AI can better understand the relationships between different types of data and produce more comprehensive, context-aware outputs.

Advantages of Multi-Modal AI

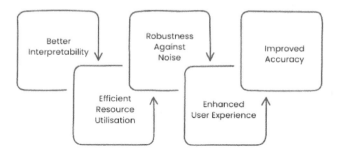

Multi-modal models are particularly useful in applications like virtual assistants, content creation, interactive media, and advanced automation systems. They allow AI to generate outputs that are not only textually coherent but also visually or audibly engaging, creating more dynamic user experiences and enabling more sophisticated problem-solving capabilities.

These technological pillars—neural networks, large language models, reinforcement learning, and multi-modal integration—form the backbone of generative AI's capabilities. Together, they enable AI to create, optimize, and innovate across a wide range of industries and applications. As these technologies continue to evolve and converge, generative AI will become increasingly powerful, offering even greater potential for transforming the way we work, create, and solve complex problems.

1.3 Strengths and Limitations of Generative AI

Generative AI has proven to be a transformative force across numerous industries, offering a wide range of benefits and capabilities that enhance productivity, creativity, and efficiency. However, like any advanced technology, it also comes with its own set of limitations and challenges. Understanding both the strengths and limitations of generative AI is crucial for businesses, policymakers, and researchers as they work to harness its potential while mitigating risks.

1.3.1 Strengths of Generative AI:

1. **Scalability**: One of the most significant advantages of generative AI is its scalability. By automating the process of creation, it enables businesses to produce large volumes of content, designs, or solutions with remarkable speed and efficiency. Whether it's generating thousands of marketing materials, developing software code, or creating new product prototypes, generative AI can rapidly iterate on ideas and produce outputs at a scale that would be impossible for human teams to match. This scalability makes it particularly valuable in industries where large-scale content creation is needed, such as advertising, entertainment, and e-commerce. As AI systems improve, they can handle more complex tasks, driving even greater efficiencies in production processes across various sectors.

2. **Personalization**: Generative AI excels in personalizing outputs based on specific inputs, contexts, or individual preferences. It can tailor content—whether text, images, or audio—based on the needs and interests of particular audiences. For example, in marketing, AI can create personalized email campaigns or product recommendations for

individual customers based on their browsing history or purchasing behavior. In education, AI can generate learning materials tailored to each student's level of understanding or learning style. This ability to customize and personalize outputs at scale allows businesses to engage customers more effectively, enhance user experiences, and provide products or services that are more aligned with individual needs.

3. **Creativity Amplification**: Generative AI serves as a powerful tool for amplifying human creativity. While it does not replace the need for human imagination, it can inspire new ideas, suggest alternatives, and generate designs that may not have been conceived otherwise. Artists, writers, designers, and other creatives can use generative AI to explore different creative directions, generate drafts or mockups, or enhance their existing work. For example, AI can propose different versions of a design, create complex music compositions, or help writers by generating plot ideas or character dialogues. By acting as a collaborative partner, generative AI can broaden the scope of what is possible, encouraging more experimentation and innovation in the creative process.

1.3.2 Limitations of Generative AI:

1. **Accuracy Issues**: Despite its impressive capabilities, generative AI is not infallible, and its outputs can sometimes suffer from significant accuracy issues. The AI systems might produce results that are incorrect, incomplete, or inconsistent, especially when the input data is ambiguous or insufficient. For example, an AI model might generate a report with factual errors or create an image that does not reflect the intended concept accurately. Additionally, generative AI models can sometimes reinforce existing biases in the data they are trained on, leading to biased outputs. These accuracy issues can be particularly problematic in domains where precision is crucial, such as healthcare, legal advice, or financial forecasting. As a result, human oversight remains necessary to ensure that AI-generated content is reliable and accurate.

2. **Context Limitations**: Generative AI models, while capable of producing impressive outputs, often struggle with understanding the deeper context or nuances of a situation. They may generate responses that appear coherent on the surface but fail to consider broader contextual factors or subtleties that

require human judgment. For example, an AI-driven customer service chatbot might provide helpful answers but may lack the emotional intelligence needed to handle sensitive or complex issues with empathy. In creative fields, an AI-generated piece might lack the emotional depth or cultural relevance that a human creator would intuitively understand. As a result, while generative AI can be a powerful tool for automation and idea generation, it often requires human oversight and intervention to ensure that the outputs are contextually appropriate and align with the desired goals or values.

3. **Ethical Concerns**: The rise of generative AI has brought with it a host of ethical challenges that require careful consideration and governance. One of the most pressing concerns is the potential for AI-generated content to be used in ways that could spread misinformation or manipulate public opinion. For instance, AI could generate realistic-looking fake news articles, social media posts, or videos that are difficult to distinguish from authentic content, contributing to the spread of false information. Similarly, generative AI models may be used to create deepfake videos or voice simulations that could be

exploited for malicious purposes, such as identity theft or defamation.

Additionally, the use of generative AI raises questions about copyright infringement and intellectual property. Since AI models are trained on vast datasets that often include copyrighted materials, there is concern about whether the content generated by AI infringes on the rights of original creators. This has implications for industries like music, art, and literature, where ownership and originality are critical issues. To address these concerns, it is essential to establish robust governance frameworks that ensure transparency, accountability, and ethical use of generative AI, including safeguards against misuse, bias, and violations of privacy.

While generative AI offers enormous potential, both in terms of innovation and productivity, its limitations must be acknowledged and addressed. By understanding these strengths and weaknesses, businesses and organizations can make more informed decisions about when and how to integrate generative AI into their operations. Ensuring that AI is used responsibly, with proper oversight and ethical guidelines, will be key to maximizing its benefits while minimizing its risks.

1.4 Real-World Examples of Business Impact

Generative AI is already making a significant impact across a wide range of industries, enabling companies to improve efficiency, innovate faster, and enhance customer experiences. Below are several notable real-world examples that showcase how businesses are leveraging generative AI to drive tangible results:

1.4.1 E-commerce Personalization

One of the most profound applications of generative AI is in **e-commerce personalization**. Companies like **Amazon** have integrated AI to create highly personalized shopping experiences for their customers. By analyzing vast amounts of data from past purchases, browsing behavior, and customer preferences, generative AI can generate tailored product recommendations that increase conversion rates and customer satisfaction. The AI models are capable of understanding intricate patterns in consumer behavior and predicting what products a customer is likely to be interested in, improving both the accuracy and relevance of product suggestions.

Beyond product recommendations, generative AI is also used to craft personalized marketing copy. This includes generating targeted emails, advertisements, and promotional content that resonate with individual customers. For example, AI can generate dynamic email subject lines, copy, and product descriptions that align with each customer's interests, increasing engagement and the likelihood of conversions.

By automating and personalizing content at scale, businesses can build stronger customer relationships and enhance loyalty without increasing manual effort.

1.4.2 Product Design

In the field of **product design**, **Autodesk** has been at the forefront of using generative AI for **rapid prototyping** in engineering and architecture. Autodesk's generative design software allows engineers and designers to input specific parameters—such as material types, weight constraints, and desired performance criteria—and then the AI generates a range of possible product designs that meet these specifications. This not only accelerates the prototyping process but also enables the creation of designs that might not be possible through traditional methods.

For example, in architecture, generative AI can propose innovative building structures that optimize space usage, energy efficiency, and aesthetic appeal, all while minimizing environmental impact.

In the manufacturing sector, generative AI can optimize the design of mechanical parts, reducing material waste and production costs while maintaining or improving the functionality and performance of the final product. The ability to explore a wide range of design alternatives in a short amount of time dramatically enhances the innovation cycle, giving companies a competitive edge in developing cutting-edge products.

1.4.3 Customer Support

Customer support is another area where generative AI is delivering immediate and substantial business benefits. Companies are increasingly turning to **chatbots** and **virtual assistants** powered by advanced generative models like **GPT** to handle complex customer queries.

These AI-driven solutions are capable of engaging in natural, contextually aware conversations with customers, providing accurate and helpful responses without requiring human intervention for most inquiries.

For example, major brands such as **Shopify** and **H&M** use AI chatbots to handle a wide range of customer service tasks, from answering product-related questions to assisting with order tracking and returns. Generative AI chatbots are designed to understand nuanced customer inquiries, allowing them to provide personalized, relevant answers based on the context of the conversation. This reduces wait times, improves the customer experience, and alleviates the burden on human support agents, enabling them to focus on more complex issues.

Additionally, generative AI-powered chatbots can operate 24/7, ensuring that businesses are able to provide consistent, high-quality support at any time, regardless of time zones or customer volume. This can lead to reduced operational costs and increased customer satisfaction.

As AI models continue to improve, the complexity of customer queries that can be handled automatically will only expand, offering even more opportunities for businesses to streamline their support operations.

1.4.4 Expanding the Business Strategy Framework with Generative AI

These examples provide a strong foundation for understanding how generative AI can be leveraged in various business sectors. However, the true potential of generative AI lies in how companies integrate these technologies into their overall strategies. To do so effectively, organizations must not only focus on individual applications like personalization, product design, or customer support but also consider how generative AI can drive innovation across their entire value chain.

For instance, in **research and development**, generative AI can be used to generate new product ideas, simulate different market scenarios, or even create entirely new business models. In **marketing**, AI can dynamically adjust advertising content to match the evolving preferences of target audiences, driving more effective campaigns. In **supply chain management**, AI can optimize inventory levels, predict demand, and generate logistics solutions that minimize costs and improve efficiency.

To maximize the impact of generative AI, organizations must ensure that it is embedded in their business strategy from the ground up. This includes investing in the necessary infrastructure, data capabilities, and talent to harness AI's full potential. Additionally, companies must focus on building ethical frameworks around AI adoption, addressing concerns related to data privacy, bias, and transparency. By thoughtfully incorporating generative AI into their strategic plans, businesses can unlock new avenues for growth, productivity, and competitive advantage, while remaining agile in a rapidly evolving technological landscape.

Chapter 2: Strategic Alignment— Mapping AI to Business Objectives

2.1 Identifying High-Impact Use Cases

To harness the full potential of generative AI, organizations must first identify the specific areas where this technology can drive substantial improvements. This process requires a deep understanding of both the internal pain points within the organization and the broader business goals. By adopting a structured, methodical approach, companies can pinpoint high-impact use cases that align with their strategic objectives and deliver measurable value. Here's an expanded breakdown of how to identify and prioritize these opportunities:

2.1.1 Stakeholder Interviews

A critical first step in identifying AI opportunities is engaging key stakeholders across the organization. These stakeholders—ranging from leadership to front-line employees—possess valuable insights into the operational inefficiencies, bottlenecks, and unmet needs that are ripe for AI-driven innovation. By conducting **interviews** or **workshops** with different teams, businesses can surface pain points that might not be immediately obvious to higher-level managers or external consultants.

For example, the sales team might identify challenges in creating personalized proposals for clients at scale, while the operations team may highlight inefficiencies in inventory management. Listening to stakeholders from various departments ensures that generative AI initiatives are grounded in real-world challenges and aligned with the needs of the business. Moreover, this approach fosters cross-functional collaboration and buy-in, ensuring that AI projects are not isolated but integrated across business units.

2.1.2 Data Inventory

Data is the lifeblood of generative AI, and assessing an organization's **data assets** is a critical next step in identifying where AI can be applied effectively. This involves evaluating the types of data available—such as customer information, transactional data, operational metrics, and content libraries—and determining how they can be leveraged for generative tasks.

For example, a retail company might have access to vast amounts of customer behavior data, product preferences, and purchase histories. These data points can be used to feed AI models that personalize product recommendations or optimize inventory management. Similarly, a company with a rich repository of design or manufacturing data can apply generative AI to accelerate product prototyping and reduce time-to-market. Understanding the data landscape helps identify where generative AI can be most effective in creating valuable, actionable insights or automating processes that would otherwise require significant human effort.

2.1.3 Customer-Centric Design

At its core, generative AI has the potential to drastically enhance customer experiences by offering more personalized, efficient, and innovative solutions. Therefore, it's essential to design AI use cases with the customer in mind. By identifying how AI can improve customer touchpoints, address pain points, or create new value propositions, organizations can prioritize initiatives that lead to better customer satisfaction and loyalty.

For instance, a company that offers subscription-based services may use generative AI to personalize content recommendations, ensuring that each customer receives tailored suggestions based on their previous interactions and preferences. Similarly, a business in the financial sector may use AI to create customized investment plans that cater to individual risk tolerances, financial goals, and market trends. Understanding customer needs—whether through direct feedback, user research, or data analysis—ensures that generative AI initiatives are not just internally efficient but also externally impactful.

2.1.4 Example Framework for Identifying AI Opportunities

Once organizations have gathered insights from stakeholders, assessed their data assets, and considered customer needs, they can begin to structure their opportunities in a clear, actionable way.

A simple framework can help map business goals to specific pain points and identify AI opportunities that are aligned with both. Here's an example framework to guide this process:

Business Goal	Pain Point	AI Opportunity
Increase Revenue	Slow product development and time-to-market	**Generative design tools** that create rapid prototypes and accelerate product development cycles.
Improve Customer Retention	Inconsistent or lackluster personalization	**AI-driven recommendation engines** that tailor content and product suggestions based on customer behavior and preferences.
Reduce Operational Costs	Manual, repetitive tasks in content creation	**Automated content generation** for marketing materials, product descriptions, or social media posts, reducing the burden on human resources and accelerating output.
Enhance Innovation	Limited ideation for new products or services	**Generative models for idea generation** that propose new features, designs, or market approaches based on emerging trends or customer data.
Boost Efficiency	Inefficient resource allocation in logistics	**AI-powered predictive analytics** that optimize supply chains, forecasting demand, and improving stock management.

This table serves as a simple yet effective method for mapping out AI opportunities in the context of business goals. By explicitly linking pain points with actionable AI solutions, organizations can create a prioritized list of use cases that deliver high-value outcomes. This approach also ensures that AI initiatives are purpose-driven and aligned with the strategic vision of the company.

2.1.5 Refining the Use Case Selection:

As organizations continue to explore and identify potential generative AI applications, it's important to refine their selection process. Here are a few criteria to consider when prioritizing use cases:

- **Return on Investment (ROI)**: Focus on AI opportunities that promise the greatest impact in terms of cost reduction, revenue generation, or efficiency improvements.

- **Feasibility**: Assess the technical and data readiness required to implement each AI use case. Some opportunities may require more advanced infrastructure or data preparation than others.

- **Scalability**: Prioritize use cases that can scale across different areas of the business or adapt to future growth.

- **Customer Impact**: Choose opportunities that directly enhance the customer experience or provide tangible value to end-users, improving satisfaction and retention.

- **Ethical Considerations**: Ensure that the selected use cases are aligned with ethical guidelines, especially in areas like data privacy, transparency, and bias mitigation.

By systematically identifying, refining, and prioritizing high-impact use cases, organizations can effectively integrate generative AI into their strategies. This ensures that AI initiatives not only align with business goals but also deliver significant, measurable outcomes that support long-term success and competitiveness.

2.2 Aligning AI Initiatives with Core Strategies

Integrating **generative AI** into an organization's operations requires a strategic approach to ensure that AI projects are not isolated efforts but are fully aligned with the company's broader business objectives. For AI initiatives to have a meaningful, long-lasting impact, they must be integrated seamlessly into the company's core strategies, driving tangible outcomes across departments and contributing to the organization's overall success. To achieve this, companies need to focus on a few key principles, such as defining success metrics and promoting cross-functional collaboration. These steps help avoid fragmented implementations and ensure that AI projects contribute to the organization's larger vision.

AI Strategy Framework

| Aligned AI Vision | Ethics & Governance | Opportunity Identification | Roadmap & Goals | Organization Enablement |

2.2.1 Defining Success Metrics

One of the fundamental challenges when implementing AI projects is ensuring that they align with **measurable business outcomes**. Without clear success metrics, it becomes difficult to evaluate the true impact of AI initiatives. Organizations must establish **Key Performance Indicators**

(KPIs) that are directly tied to their business objectives, ensuring that AI projects contribute to measurable improvements in key areas like revenue growth, customer satisfaction, or operational efficiency.

For instance, if the goal of an AI project is to **increase sales**, the success metric could be the percentage increase in revenue from AI-driven recommendations or personalized content. If the focus is on improving **time-to-market**, success could be measured by the reduction in product development cycle time achieved through generative design tools or automated testing. Defining clear KPIs helps business leaders track the progress of AI initiatives, ensuring they are delivering the expected value and contributing to organizational goals.

Moreover, defining success metrics requires businesses to set both **short-term and long-term goals** for AI projects. Short-term metrics might focus on immediate improvements, such as reducing manual workloads or automating routine tasks, while long-term metrics might look at more strategic outcomes, such as fostering innovation, expanding market share, or improving overall business agility. This dual approach ensures that AI is delivering both immediate operational benefits and contributing to long-term strategic goals.

2.2.2 Cross-Functional Collaboration

AI projects are most effective when they are not developed in isolation by a single department but are driven by **collaboration across the organization**. To fully harness the power of generative AI, it is essential to break down traditional silos and encourage **cross-functional teamwork** from the outset.

This includes involving stakeholders from **technology, marketing, operations, sales**, and **customer service** teams early in the project lifecycle. Each of these departments brings unique perspectives that can inform the successful design and implementation of AI solutions.

For example, **technology teams** are essential in providing the technical expertise required for AI model development, while **marketing teams** can ensure that the AI solutions align with customer preferences and drive business outcomes.

Operations teams can provide insight into areas where AI can optimize workflows, reduce costs, or improve service efficiency. By engaging cross-functional teams, organizations can ensure that the AI initiatives are addressing real-world business challenges and are feasible from both a technical and operational standpoint.

Example of AI Cross-functional Collaboration

Incorporating diverse perspectives also helps mitigate risks. For example, marketing and customer support teams can help identify potential **ethical concerns** related to AI applications, such as issues with data privacy or customer trust. Technology and operations teams can provide feedback on the **technical feasibility** and the potential for **scalability**, ensuring that AI solutions are not only effective in the short term but also capable of expanding as the business grows.

Furthermore, this collaboration fosters a sense of shared ownership and accountability, which is critical for the success of AI initiatives. When teams from various departments are aligned and working toward a common goal, they can collectively contribute to refining the AI project, adjusting the approach as needed, and ensuring successful deployment across the organization.

2.2.3 Aligning AI with Business Goals

Aligning AI initiatives with business goals requires that organizations move beyond simply implementing technology for the sake of innovation and instead focus on how AI can directly contribute to the business's **mission and vision**. AI should be seen as a tool to drive business success, whether it's improving operational efficiency, creating new customer experiences, or enhancing decision-making capabilities.

For instance, if a company's overarching goal is to **increase market share** in a competitive industry, AI projects might focus on **enhancing customer experience** through personalized recommendations, predictive analytics, and targeted marketing campaigns. If the company is striving for **cost reduction**, AI could be implemented in **supply chain optimization**, automating inventory management, and reducing waste in manufacturing. In both cases, AI projects should be designed with the business goals in mind, ensuring that the technology directly supports the company's strategic vision.

By aligning AI projects with core business strategies, companies can ensure that AI does not become an isolated or fragmented effort but is deeply integrated into their overall business operations.

This approach also encourages the responsible and ethical use of AI, as projects are constantly evaluated against broader organizational goals, ensuring they contribute positively to the business's success.

Alignment of AI Goals with Business Objectives

| ① Define Clear Business Objectives | ② Identify AI Opportunities | ③ Quantify Value | ④ Develop Strategic AI Roadmap | ⑤ Integrate AI & Data Strategies | ⑥ Build AI & Data Literacy & Culture | ⑦ Monitor, Evaluate & Iterate |

2.2.4 Establishing a Governance Framework

As part of aligning AI initiatives with business strategies, companies must also establish a **governance framework** to ensure that AI projects are conducted ethically and responsibly. This framework should include policies on data privacy, bias mitigation, and transparency.

Clear governance structures help ensure that AI solutions are used in a way that aligns with company values and regulatory requirements, thereby reducing potential risks and ensuring the AI project's long-term sustainability.

This governance framework can also define clear roles and responsibilities for stakeholders, ensuring that there is continuous oversight and accountability throughout the AI project lifecycle. It helps ensure that cross-functional teams not only work together to meet business goals but also adhere to the necessary ethical standards and legal requirements.

2.2.5 Measuring and Refining AI Impact

Once AI initiatives are aligned with core business strategies, it's important to continually measure their impact and refine the approach over time.

Success metrics, as discussed earlier, should be tracked regularly to ensure that AI initiatives are delivering on their objectives.

However, businesses must also be agile and flexible, adjusting their AI strategy as new challenges or opportunities arise. This iterative process of measurement, feedback, and refinement is key to ensuring that AI solutions remain relevant and impactful as the organization's needs evolve.

By continuously evaluating AI initiatives against business goals and KPIs, organizations can ensure that their AI projects are not only delivering immediate benefits but are also contributing to sustainable growth and innovation in the long term.

2.3 Prioritization Frameworks

When implementing generative AI in an organization, it's essential to recognize that not all potential use cases are of equal value or importance. Given the complexity and resources required for AI projects, it's crucial to focus on initiatives that not only offer the greatest **business value** but are also **feasible** and come with manageable risks.

A structured **prioritization framework** helps decision-makers assess various AI opportunities in a systematic way, ensuring that the organization invests its time and resources in the most impactful projects. One effective method for prioritizing AI initiatives is through a **scoring system** that evaluates use cases across three primary criteria: **impact potential, feasibility,** and **risk level**.

2.3.1 Impact Potential

The first step in prioritizing AI use cases is to assess the **impact potential** of each initiative. This refers to the extent to which the AI project can drive tangible, measurable outcomes for the business. The **impact potential** can be broken down into several key factors:

- **Revenue Growth**: Will the AI project contribute to increasing sales, entering new markets, or improving customer retention? Projects that have a direct or indirect link to **revenue generation** are often high-priority because they align with the organization's growth objectives. For example, implementing an AI-powered recommendation engine in an e-commerce platform could lead to higher sales by offering customers personalized product suggestions.

- **Cost Savings**: AI can be a powerful tool for **cost optimization** by automating repetitive tasks, improving supply chain efficiency, or reducing waste in production. A use case that significantly reduces costs—for example, an AI model that optimizes inventory management—can have a high impact on the bottom line. These initiatives not only improve profitability but also create the room for reinvestment into more strategic areas of the business.

- **Innovation Boost**: Some AI initiatives may not have an immediate revenue impact but could drive long-term innovation. For instance, applying generative AI in product design could enable a company to create groundbreaking products that redefine market offerings or open new business opportunities. These types of projects can provide substantial **competitive advantage** over time by positioning the organization as a leader in its industry.

By assessing the **impact potential** of various use cases, companies can prioritize AI projects that promise the greatest rewards in terms of revenue, cost reduction, or innovation.

2.3.2 Feasibility

While impact is crucial, the feasibility of implementing an AI solution is equally important. A promising AI project may not be worth pursuing if it's not technically **feasible** or if the organization lacks the necessary **resources** to execute it. To assess **feasibility**, consider the following factors:

- **Data Availability**: AI projects are data-driven, meaning that the quality and quantity of available data is a critical factor in determining feasibility. If a use case requires large datasets or specific types of data (such as customer behavior data for personalized recommendations), the organization must first evaluate whether this data is readily accessible and of sufficient quality. For example, a generative AI model for predicting customer preferences in real-time requires robust customer interaction data that may not always be available or may need to be collected.

- **Technical Complexity**: The complexity of the AI solution itself plays a significant role in determining whether a project can be realistically executed. Some AI models, particularly deep learning models or highly specialized generative algorithms, can require substantial technical expertise and significant computational power. Simpler models or those with readily available frameworks (like GPT-based language models) may be easier to implement but may not always provide the desired results. Assessing the **technical complexity** helps determine if the organization's team has the skills or if there is a need to partner with external vendors or specialists.

- **Resource Requirements**: Even if an AI use case is technically feasible, it's essential to evaluate whether the company has the resources to execute it. This includes human capital (e.g., data scientists, engineers, or AI specialists), financial capital (e.g., for tools, software licenses, or computing power), and time (e.g., how long it will take to develop, test, and deploy the AI solution). Projects that require extensive resources may need to be prioritized carefully or delayed until the necessary resources are available.

By assessing feasibility across these areas, organizations can ensure that they are investing in AI projects that are technically viable and realistically achievable within their existing infrastructure and capabilities.

2.3.3 Risk Level

No AI project comes without risks, and understanding the potential risks associated with each initiative is critical to informed decision-making. AI projects can carry various types of risks, and a proper **risk assessment** helps organizations mitigate these before proceeding. The major types of risks to consider include:

- **Ethical Risks**: Generative AI projects, in particular, can introduce ethical challenges, such as potential biases in AI outputs or the creation of content that could mislead users. For instance, if an AI tool is trained on biased data, it could generate recommendations that unfairly favor one demographic over another, perpetuating inequality. It's important to assess whether an AI initiative has **ethical implications** and whether safeguards can be put in place to mitigate these risks, such as implementing bias detection mechanisms or ensuring transparency in AI decision-making.

- **Regulatory Risks**: AI solutions, particularly those involving customer data, are subject to **regulations** related to data privacy and security, such as the GDPR in Europe or CCPA in California. It's essential to consider whether the proposed AI use case complies with the applicable legal frameworks and whether there are potential legal ramifications or penalties for non-compliance. AI projects in highly regulated industries—such as healthcare or finance—may face stricter regulations that must be carefully navigated.

- **Operational Risks**: AI initiatives can also introduce operational risks. These might include the potential for **system failures**, the need for ongoing maintenance, or the risk that the AI model might not perform as expected. Furthermore, integrating AI into existing workflows can sometimes disrupt business operations or require retraining of staff. These operational risks should be carefully assessed to ensure that the AI implementation process doesn't negatively impact other areas of the business.

By evaluating the **risk level** associated with each AI use case, organizations can prioritize those projects that offer the highest reward with the lowest possible risk. In some cases, organizations might choose to mitigate risk by starting with smaller pilot projects or collaborating with external experts.

2.3.4 Example Scoring System:

To make the prioritization process more objective, a simple scoring system can be used. For each use case, assign a score from 1 to 5 for each criterion—impact potential, feasibility, and risk level—and then calculate an overall score. Here's an example:

Use Case	Impact Potential	Feasibility	Risk Level	Total Score
AI-driven product recommen- dations	5	4	2	11
Automated customer support chatbots	4	5	3	12
Generative design for R&D	4	3	4	11

The use case with the highest total score—**automated customer support chatbots**—would be prioritized as it offers the best balance between high impact, feasibility, and manageable risk.

Key Takeaway:

Using a prioritization framework that considers **impact potential**, **feasibility**, and **risk level** helps organizations ensure that their AI investments deliver the highest value. It provides a structured way to assess different initiatives and allocate resources effectively, ensuring that the most promising, high-reward AI projects are pursued first. Through careful evaluation and prioritization, businesses can achieve successful AI outcomes while minimizing unnecessary risks.

2.4 Risk Assessment and Mitigation Strategies

Generative AI, while a powerful tool, introduces several unique risks that organizations must carefully assess and mitigate to ensure the technology is used responsibly and effectively. These risks range from **technical issues** such as hallucination errors (where the AI generates false or nonsensical outputs), to **ethical concerns** like unintended biases, and even **legal risks**, such as intellectual property (IP) violations.

Given these challenges, it is crucial for organizations to put in place comprehensive **risk management** and **mitigation**

strategies to prevent or reduce these risks, ensuring that AI deployment leads to positive and sustainable outcomes.

2.4.1 Bias Audits

One of the most significant concerns with generative AI models is **bias**. Since these models are trained on vast datasets that often reflect societal inequalities, there is a risk that AI systems might inadvertently perpetuate or amplify biases related to gender, race, socioeconomic status, or other factors. This can result in **discriminatory outcomes** that harm individuals or groups, especially when AI is used for tasks such as hiring, loan approval, or healthcare diagnosis.

To mitigate these risks, organizations must conduct **bias audits** regularly. A bias audit involves evaluating the data used to train AI models to identify potential sources of bias, as well as testing the AI outputs for signs of discrimination or unfair treatment.

The audit should also focus on ensuring that the AI models are inclusive and equitable, not just technically accurate. For example, when implementing a generative AI model for creating marketing materials, businesses should check if the AI-generated content is inadvertently favoring one demographic group over another, and take steps to correct these biases.

What is AI Bias Audit?

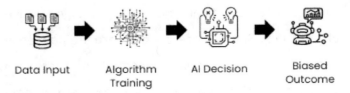

Data Input   Algorithm Training   AI Decision   Biased Outcome

Moreover, audits should be ongoing, not just a one-time process. As AI models are continuously refined and retrained with new data, it is critical to ensure that any changes in the model's behavior are also checked for new biases. This proactive approach helps reduce the risk of **reputational damage**, **legal challenges**, and **loss of trust** from customers, especially in industries with sensitive applications.

2.4.2 Human Oversight

Another key strategy to mitigate the risks of generative AI is ensuring **human oversight** in the decision-making process. While AI can produce impressive results, it is still prone to errors or limitations that may not align with the values or expectations of a business or its customers. For example, generative AI models might produce **hallucinated outputs**— information that appears plausible but is entirely fabricated. In high-stakes situations, such as medical or financial decision-making, such errors can have serious consequences.

To address this risk, AI outputs should be used as **augmented tools**, not standalone solutions. This means that humans should remain involved in critical decisions, reviewing and verifying AI-generated outputs before they are implemented.

For instance, an AI system used for content creation should be checked by human editors to ensure the text is coherent, factually accurate, and culturally appropriate. Similarly, AI-generated design ideas or marketing strategies should undergo human review to ensure they align with brand values and customer expectations.

By maintaining human oversight, organizations can take advantage of AI's capabilities while ensuring that the technology remains under control and aligned with business and ethical standards. This oversight can also help catch errors that may not be apparent to the AI model itself, such as misunderstandings of context or unintended consequences in customer interactions.

2.4.3 Regulatory Compliance

As generative AI technologies continue to evolve, so too do the **regulatory frameworks** that govern their use. Organizations must stay ahead of **legal requirements** related to AI deployment, especially in sectors that are heavily regulated, such as healthcare, finance, and education. Non-compliance with local and international regulations can result in **severe legal consequences**, including fines, sanctions, and reputational damage.

To mitigate regulatory risks, businesses should establish a framework for continuous monitoring of relevant laws and regulations. This includes understanding the implications of data protection laws (like the **General Data Protection Regulation (GDPR)** in the EU), intellectual property rights, and the use of AI in specific industries. For example, in healthcare, the **Health Insurance Portability and Accountability Act (HIPAA)** in the United States dictates how personal health data can be used and shared, which must be taken into consideration when implementing AI for healthcare applications.

Moreover, organizations should be transparent with stakeholders about their AI systems and how they collect, use, and store data. **Audit trails** should be maintained to document the decision-making process and ensure accountability. When AI systems are used in customer-facing applications, businesses must provide **clear disclosures** about how AI is being used and obtain **informed consent** where necessary.

Staying proactive about compliance ensures that AI technologies can be deployed without legal interruptions and that the organization is prepared to adapt to any changes in regulatory environments.

Having a **legal advisory team** specialized in AI-related issues can help businesses remain compliant, understand potential risks, and implement best practices for responsible AI use.

2.4.4 Transparency and Explainability

Transparency and **explainability** are key aspects of mitigating risks related to AI, particularly when it comes to ensuring trust from customers and regulators.

Many AI models, especially deep learning-based generative models, operate as **black boxes**, meaning their decision-making processes are not easily understandable to humans. This lack of transparency can be problematic, especially when AI systems are involved in sensitive decisions.

To mitigate this risk, organizations should prioritize the development of AI models that are **explainable**—meaning that their decision-making process can be clearly articulated and understood by human users. This is particularly important in industries like finance or healthcare, where AI outputs can have significant real-world consequences. For example, if an AI model is used to assist in loan approval decisions, the model's reasoning for rejecting or approving an application should be transparent to both customers and regulators.

Investing in explainable AI (XAI) tools and methodologies can help organizations make AI outputs more understandable and trustworthy. Furthermore, fostering **transparency** about AI processes can reduce the risk of customers feeling manipulated or deceived by AI technologies.

2.4.5 Intellectual Property (IP) Protection

Generative AI also raises concerns related to **intellectual property (IP)**, particularly when AI creates content that may resemble existing works, potentially infringing on copyrights, patents, or trademarks. Organizations need to ensure that their AI-generated outputs do not violate the IP rights of others or create IP challenges for themselves.

To mitigate these risks, businesses should ensure that they have a clear understanding of how AI models are trained and the sources of data used. This includes ensuring that training data is **legally sourced** and does not infringe on third-party IP. Additionally, companies should establish clear policies around the ownership of AI-generated content.

For example, if an AI system creates a piece of artwork or a piece of music, the business should have a clear policy in place regarding who owns the rights to that content and how it can be used commercially.

Generative AI offers immense potential for innovation, but it also introduces a range of risks that need to be carefully managed. By implementing robust **bias audits**, maintaining **human oversight**, staying compliant with **regulatory frameworks**, prioritizing **transparency and explainability**, and safeguarding against **IP violations**, organizations can mitigate these risks and ensure that their AI initiatives are responsible, ethical, and successful.

A proactive approach to risk management not only helps businesses avoid pitfalls but also builds trust with stakeholders and customers, ensuring that generative AI can be used to its full potential in a way that benefits both the organization and society at large.

Chapter 3: Talent and Capability Development

As the potential of generative AI grows, it's becoming increasingly clear that the success of AI transformation within any organization depends not only on the technology itself but also on the capabilities and mindset of its workforce.

AI can automate processes, generate insights, and enhance decision-making, but for these tools to be used effectively and responsibly, organizations must ensure that their teams are equipped with the right skills, knowledge, and mindset to leverage the full power of AI.

Building and nurturing the right talent is crucial, but it is equally important to create a **culture and environment** that encourages continuous learning, creativity, and collaboration. This chapter delves into the critical strategies for developing an **AI-ready workforce**, **upskilling** existing teams, **attracting** and **retaining** top AI talent, and fostering a **culture of innovation** that ensures long-term success in the AI-driven future.

3.1 Building an AI-Ready Workforce

The journey to AI-driven business transformation begins with human capital. For organizations to successfully leverage generative AI technologies, they must first build a workforce equipped with the necessary skills, knowledge, and mindset. An AI-ready workforce doesn't just mean hiring new talent; it involves reshaping the existing workforce, aligning them with AI initiatives, and equipping them with the tools to work alongside AI systems effectively.

This process requires a commitment to long-term investment in people, fostering a culture that supports growth, adaptability, and continuous learning. The workforce needs to evolve to integrate AI into everyday business operations, not just as a technological tool, but as a core part of how work is done and value is delivered.

Developing an AI-ready workforce ensures the organization remains competitive and is capable of adapting to the rapidly evolving landscape of artificial intelligence.

3.1.1 Leadership Training in AI Fundamentals

Organizational transformation with AI begins at the top. Senior leaders must have a fundamental understanding of AI technologies, their potential, and limitations to guide the company's strategic direction effectively.

While they may not need to become experts, understanding the basics allows them to make informed decisions about resource allocation, project priorities, and business alignment with AI initiatives. Leaders must recognize that AI is not merely a tool but a strategic asset that will shape the company's future.

For this to happen, leadership training must be a priority. AI training programs should be designed to provide high-level overviews of machine learning, deep learning, natural language processing, and ethical considerations. These training sessions allow leaders to understand the **strategic potential** of AI and **evaluate its impact** on different aspects of the business, from operations to marketing, finance, and customer service. Leaders should also learn to identify the challenges and risks of AI deployment, ensuring they can approach AI projects with both optimism and caution. This training not only helps in making more informed decisions but also sets the tone for the rest of the organization in embracing AI-driven change.

3.1.2 Cross-Departmental Skill Development

AI isn't just a concern for the tech or data teams—its impact spans the entire organization. Successful implementation requires that knowledge of AI be embedded across all departments. Therefore, it's vital to upskill employees across different functions.

The marketing team might need to understand AI-driven customer segmentation, while the operations team needs to grasp how AI can optimize workflows and reduce inefficiencies. No department can afford to be isolated from the impact of AI, and each team should recognize how AI can enhance its specific responsibilities.

Upskilling employees across various functions ensures that AI is adopted not just as a tech-driven initiative, but as a business-wide transformation. When employees from departments like marketing, sales, finance, or human resources gain a foundational understanding of AI, they can identify opportunities for using AI in their own work, improving efficiency and innovation.

Customizing training to meet the specific needs of each department allows teams to understand how AI directly affects their day-to-day tasks, leading to higher engagement and a sense of ownership over AI initiatives.

This company-wide approach to upskilling fosters a deeper level of collaboration between departments, driving the full potential of AI and leading to synergies that benefit the business as a whole.

3.1.3 Structured Learning Paths

Not all employees have the same level of technical expertise. Structured, scalable learning paths should be developed to accommodate everyone from beginners to advanced practitioners.

For those just starting out, foundational courses on data science, machine learning, and AI ethics should be offered, while more advanced professionals should receive training in specific applications of AI, such as natural language processing or neural networks. These learning paths should cater to a diverse audience with varying levels of expertise, allowing everyone to start at a level appropriate to their current knowledge base.

Structured learning paths, with clear milestones and certifications, give employees a sense of progression and accomplishment. Employees should be encouraged to pursue both **theoretical** and **practical learning**. For example, hands-on projects and challenges integrated into the training curriculum will enable employees to directly apply what they've learned in real-world scenarios. These projects can span a range of applications, from building simple predictive models to creating AI-driven marketing campaigns or designing AI-optimized supply chains. By incorporating practical learning into the curriculum, companies ensure that their employees not only understand AI concepts but can confidently apply them in their roles.

3.1.4 Creating Organizational AI Fluency

AI fluency should be an essential part of your organizational culture. While technical roles will need deep expertise, other roles should understand how AI works and how to apply it in their day-to-day functions.

This broad **AI fluency** ensures everyone in the organization is aligned and able to communicate effectively about AI's capabilities, benefits, and challenges. It's no longer enough to have a few technical experts on staff; every employee should understand the language of AI, even if they don't work directly with the technology. This broader understanding fosters collaboration between teams and departments, ensuring that

AI projects are better aligned with business objectives and that their full potential is realized.

For instance, HR professionals might benefit from understanding AI-driven talent analytics to make more informed hiring decisions, while customer service teams can leverage AI tools for automation and enhanced customer interactions.

AI literacy helps departments across the organization communicate effectively about AI projects, ensuring a unified approach to adoption and use. Additionally, **AI fluency** in non-technical roles helps to dispel common misconceptions about AI, fostering a more open-minded and positive reception to AI-driven changes.

Regular workshops, internal seminars, and webinars can help integrate AI literacy into the fabric of the organization, ensuring no team is left behind. These sessions can be designed to showcase real-world examples of how AI is being used within the company, as well as highlight successful case studies from other industries.

By making AI a company-wide priority, organizations can create a workforce that is not only ready to embrace AI but is also equipped to lead the charge in leveraging AI for greater business impact. This holistic approach to AI literacy ensures that all employees are not only informed but motivated to take part in the AI transformation journey.

Executive AI Fluency

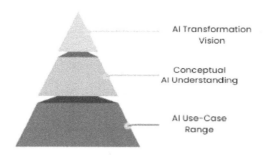

AI Transformation Vision

Conceptual AI Understanding

AI Use-Case Range

3.2 Upskilling Existing Teams

While new hires will play a crucial role in AI transformation, investing in the existing workforce is equally important. Upskilling current employees not only fosters loyalty but also allows organizations to retain valuable institutional knowledge that new hires lack. Existing teams understand the company culture, processes, and customer needs, making them well-positioned to apply AI in ways that directly address the organization's goals.

A tailored and comprehensive upskilling strategy is essential for empowering teams to embrace AI and apply it effectively, driving innovation from within. By focusing on developing the skills of current employees, companies also minimize turnover risks, reducing the time and cost spent on recruiting and onboarding new staff.

A workforce that is continuously evolving in its capabilities is better prepared for future challenges and opportunities, thus contributing to long-term success in the age of AI.

3.2.1 Data Literacy as a Foundation

Data is the backbone of AI, and fostering a data-literate workforce is the first step toward AI readiness. Employees across all departments must understand how to interpret data, spot trends, and know how data feeds into machine learning models.

As AI increasingly relies on data-driven insights to make decisions, employees who are comfortable working with data are crucial to the organization's ability to leverage AI effectively. This foundational knowledge should be provided across the board—whether employees work in sales, operations, or customer service, they need to understand how to use data to drive decisions and improve outcomes.

Data literacy programs should cover fundamental concepts such as the types of data collected, data cleaning processes, methods for ensuring data accuracy, and basic statistical analysis. These programs should not aim to turn every employee into a data scientist but rather ensure that all employees can comfortably work with data in their daily tasks.

This knowledge is key to fostering a collaborative environment in which teams can effectively communicate the value of AI applications and contribute to shaping data-driven strategies. Additionally, this broad data awareness ensures that employees will better understand how their work feeds into the broader AI processes, allowing them to align their efforts with organizational goals and improve overall decision-making.

3.2.2 Specialized AI Training

For employees in roles that are more directly involved with AI technologies, specialized training is key. Data scientists, engineers, and AI developers, for example, need to stay ahead of the curve on emerging AI methodologies, algorithms, and best practices.

AI is a rapidly evolving field, and staying updated on new developments is essential for ensuring that employees possess the cutting-edge skills needed to drive innovation and maintain a competitive edge. Specialized training should not only focus on foundational AI concepts but also include deep dives into advanced topics like reinforcement learning, neural networks, and deep learning.

In addition to formal training courses, employees should be encouraged to participate in AI-focused conferences, hackathons, and research collaborations, which help them stay up-to-date with the latest advancements in the field and gain exposure to different perspectives on AI application.

For non-technical teams, the focus should be on understanding how AI can optimize their tasks. For instance, marketing teams could learn how to use AI for predictive analytics, customer segmentation, and content generation, enabling them to create more personalized and effective marketing campaigns.

Similarly, customer service teams might focus on using AI tools to automate inquiries, handle routine questions, and improve response times, freeing up human agents to focus on more complex issues. Specialized AI training for non-technical roles ensures that all teams are equipped with the skills to adopt AI in a way that enhances productivity and improves business outcomes across the organization.

3.2.3 Hands-On Learning with AI Tools

Learning by doing is one of the most effective ways to integrate AI into the workflow. To this end, employees should be given the opportunity to experiment with AI tools, frameworks, and platforms in practical settings. Hands-on projects should be incorporated into training programs, allowing employees to apply what they've learned in real-world scenarios.

This could involve designing basic AI models, testing algorithms, or implementing pre-existing solutions to address specific business challenges. Practical application of AI skills helps bridge the gap between theoretical knowledge and actual use cases, ensuring that employees feel confident in their ability to contribute to AI initiatives.

AI sandboxes—test environments where employees can safely experiment with AI tools without the risk of disrupting core business operations—are valuable for this purpose. These sandbox environments allow employees to explore and test AI models, try out different data sets, and experiment with machine learning algorithms in a risk-free setting.

By providing access to such sandboxes, organizations enable employees to develop hands-on experience and gain practical skills that can be translated directly into their day-to-day roles. These safe testing environments also encourage employees to experiment, learn from mistakes, and innovate, accelerating the process of AI adoption and creating a more agile, responsive workforce.

3.2.4 Mentorship Programs

Experienced AI professionals can serve as mentors to less experienced employees, facilitating faster knowledge transfer and smoother adoption of AI practices. By creating a mentorship program, organizations ensure that AI expertise is spread across the business, fostering a culture of peer learning and collaboration.

These mentorships help demystify AI concepts and provide guidance on best practices, addressing challenges that employees may face when working with AI in a practical setting. Additionally, mentorships allow employees to learn from real-world experiences, gain insight into the latest trends, and understand how AI can be effectively applied within the context of their specific roles.

Mentorship programs can be formal or informal, depending on the organization's culture, but they should aim to provide guidance on practical challenges, offer advice on career progression in AI, and help mentees navigate the complex world of AI applications. By nurturing AI talent through mentorship, organizations build a strong internal network of experts who can collaborate on projects, offer support, and share best practices.

These programs also help develop leadership in AI, ensuring that the organization is cultivating a pipeline of talent capable of driving AI innovation long into the future. A mentorship program fosters an environment of continuous learning, where employees feel supported in their career development and are encouraged to contribute to the organization's AI strategy.

3.3 Attracting and Retaining AI Talent

In today's highly competitive job market, where the demand for AI experts far exceeds the supply, attracting and retaining the right talent has become one of the most critical challenges for organizations.

Generative AI, in particular, demands specialized skills that few professionals possess, and companies must build comprehensive talent strategies to stay competitive and drive AI-driven innovation. Beyond simply hiring technical experts, organizations must create environments that foster growth, collaboration, and long-term commitment to attract and keep top-tier talent.

3.3.1 Building a Strong Employer Brand in AI

Attracting top AI talent begins with developing a reputation as an innovator in the AI space. Professionals in the AI field are drawn to organizations that are at the forefront of technological advancements, particularly those that are leveraging AI to create meaningful impact.

To capture the attention of high-caliber AI professionals, it is essential for organizations to highlight the exciting AI projects they are working on, the cutting-edge technologies they are utilizing, and the tangible impact their AI initiatives are having on the industry and society at large.

Showcasing your organization's AI success stories, particularly those that demonstrate the real-world value of your projects, can establish your company as a leader in AI adoption. AI professionals are often motivated by the opportunity to work on complex, high-impact problems. By promoting the role of AI in driving business transformation within your organization, you can position your company as a destination for AI talent who want to be part of meaningful, innovative work that pushes the boundaries of what's possible with technology. Additionally, emphasizing your commitment to ethical AI practices is important, as many AI professionals want to ensure their work contributes positively to society.

3.3.2 Competitive Compensation and Benefits

While salary remains a key factor in attracting AI talent, it's not the only consideration for top professionals in the field. AI specialists are not only looking for competitive pay but also for environments where they can make an impact, grow professionally, and explore new opportunities.

A robust compensation package should, of course, reflect the market value of AI talent, but organizations should also emphasize the broader value propositions they offer, such as career progression, opportunities for innovation, and access to cutting-edge research and development.

Offering perks like equity options, flexible work arrangements, and generous benefits is important for attracting AI professionals. However, just as crucial is the ability to provide career advancement opportunities that allow AI talent to grow in their roles. AI professionals are often highly motivated by the prospect of gaining new skills, developing expertise, and taking on leadership responsibilities.

By offering opportunities to contribute to impactful projects, collaborate with other industry experts, and play a central role in shaping the AI strategy within the organization, companies can create an environment where top AI talent feels engaged and valued.

3.3.3 Creating a Dynamic, Inclusive Workplace

Diversity and inclusion are not just buzzwords but essential pillars for the successful development of AI technologies. AI thrives in diverse environments, where multiple perspectives and experiences contribute to creative and innovative problem-solving. Companies looking to attract and retain the best AI talent must actively foster a culture of inclusion where everyone feels valued, respected, and empowered to contribute their unique perspectives.

AI professionals, particularly those in underrepresented groups, are increasingly seeking out workplaces that prioritize inclusion and diversity. By integrating diversity into the recruitment and retention strategy, organizations can access a wider pool of AI talent and cultivate teams that bring diverse viewpoints, which leads to more effective and holistic AI solutions.

AI professionals want to work in environments where they can not only grow professionally but also be part of a community that values different backgrounds, experiences, and ideas. An inclusive work culture also boosts employee satisfaction, loyalty, and creativity, all of which are essential for retaining talent in the long term.

3.3.4 Opportunities for Career Development

AI professionals are often driven by a passion for pushing the boundaries of the field and tackling complex challenges. To retain top AI talent, organizations must offer clear, structured career development paths that allow these professionals to evolve as technologists, researchers, and leaders. Retaining AI talent goes beyond offering competitive salaries—it involves providing opportunities for growth, professional advancement, and leadership development.

Clear opportunities for career progression, such as pathways into senior technical roles, research positions, or leadership positions, help motivate AI professionals to stay and develop within the organization. Offering leadership development programs, mentorship opportunities, and exposure to cutting-edge projects can give AI talent the chance to expand their skill set and take on new challenges. Providing opportunities to collaborate with external thought leaders, participate in industry collaborations, or engage in AI-focused conferences and seminars can also help keep talent engaged and connected to the broader AI ecosystem.

In addition, working on high-profile, impactful AI projects allows professionals to feel that their contributions are shaping the future of AI. Companies that recognize the importance of continuous learning, provide access to training programs, and support participation in AI-related events and workshops can build long-term loyalty and enhance employee satisfaction.

When AI professionals see opportunities for ongoing career development and meaningful work, they are more likely to stay engaged and committed to the organization's goals, ensuring the long-term success of the AI transformation.

3.4 Creating a Culture of Innovation and Continuous Learning

For AI to achieve its full potential within an organization, it must be more than just a technological investment—it needs to become a fundamental part of the company's overall culture and innovation strategy. To truly harness the transformative power of AI, organizations must cultivate an environment that supports continuous learning, encourages experimentation, and fosters collaboration across departments.

AI should be integrated into the organization's core values and everyday practices, ensuring that it becomes a driver of innovation rather than simply a set of tools or systems to be applied intermittently.

3.4.1 Encourage Experimentation and Risk-Taking

Innovation in AI, as in any emerging technology, is rarely a straight path. It often involves trial, error, and the willingness to take risks. By fostering an organizational mindset that views failure as a stepping stone rather than a setback, companies can empower their teams to take calculated risks and experiment with new AI models, algorithms, and approaches. This willingness to experiment can unlock unexpected solutions to business problems and foster a deeper understanding of AI's potential.

Encouraging risk-taking not only leads to innovation but also creates a space where employees are motivated to explore new applications of AI that could be game-changers for the organization. Whether it's trying out a new machine learning technique, using AI in an unconventional area of the business, or testing an innovative customer service chatbot, the freedom to fail forward leads to valuable insights and breakthroughs. Organizations that support this kind of culture create an environment where employees are not afraid to push the boundaries of what AI can do.

3.4.2 Fostering Collaboration Across Departments

AI's interdisciplinary nature means it has the potential to impact virtually every department within an organization, from marketing to operations to HR. However, the development and successful implementation of AI solutions require collaboration across these diverse areas of expertise. For instance, data scientists and AI specialists may work alongside marketing teams to create personalized customer experiences or with product managers to develop AI-driven features.

Creating an environment where collaboration between departments is not just encouraged but actively supported is crucial. This cross-functional teamwork allows AI initiatives to align more closely with business goals and ensures that AI solutions are designed with input from those who understand the nuances of different business functions.

It also leads to more creative and holistic solutions, as different teams bring their perspectives and challenges to the table. By facilitating and promoting such interdisciplinary collaboration, organizations can accelerate the adoption of AI and ensure that its benefits are realized across the business.

3.4.3 Promote Knowledge Sharing

In order for AI to be successfully integrated into an organization, it's essential that knowledge is shared freely across all levels of the company. One of the greatest challenges for organizations implementing AI is ensuring that the expertise and insights gathered by a small group of specialists or data scientists are accessible to all relevant stakeholders. Knowledge-sharing initiatives—such as internal presentations, workshops, forums, or cross-departmental meetings—can help democratize AI knowledge and ensure that the entire organization benefits from AI advancements.

This knowledge-sharing approach encourages employees to stay updated on the latest AI trends, learn from each other's experiences, and identify best practices that can be applied across departments.

By establishing mechanisms for continuous education and collaboration, the organization not only cultivates a stronger, more AI-fluent workforce but also helps to create an environment where AI knowledge is integrated into day-to-day decision-making processes at every level of the company. It also enables employees to take ownership of AI projects, as they can draw from the expertise and ideas of their colleagues in different parts of the organization.

3.4.4 Embedding AI in Organizational Strategy

For AI to have a lasting impact, it must be embedded deeply into the organization's strategy and vision. Rather than treating AI as a separate, one-off project, it should be integrated into the company's broader goals and objectives. AI must be seen not just as a tool to solve specific problems but as a strategic enabler that drives transformation across business functions.

Embedding AI into the fabric of organizational strategy means aligning AI initiatives with the company's long-term vision, ensuring that AI efforts are coordinated with other strategic initiatives. This involves setting clear objectives for AI adoption, measuring progress through key performance indicators (KPIs), and establishing cross-functional teams that ensure AI is implemented in a way that delivers tangible value to the business. By incorporating AI into the overall business strategy, organizations can ensure that they are agile and adaptable, ready to capitalize on new AI developments as they emerge and ensuring that AI remains a key driver of innovation and growth.

When AI is considered a fundamental component of the company's strategic roadmap, it allows for continuous improvement, ensuring the business remains competitive in an increasingly AI-driven world. This long-term commitment to AI allows companies to build a culture of innovation that permeates all aspects of the organization, resulting in better decision-making, more efficient processes, and a stronger ability to meet evolving customer demands.

Building an AI-ready workforce is not a one-time initiative but an ongoing, multi-dimensional effort. By prioritizing leadership training, cross-departmental upskilling, attracting top talent, and creating a culture of continuous innovation, organizations can ensure that they not only adapt to AI but thrive with it. The key is to create an environment where talent can develop, collaborate, and continually learn in tandem with AI's rapid advancements. By doing so, you set the stage for sustainable AI adoption and innovation across your organization.

Chapter 4: Technology Integration and Infrastructure

The successful adoption of generative AI technologies within a business is not solely reliant on the availability of a skilled workforce; it also demands a robust and flexible technological infrastructure capable of supporting the complexity and demands of these advanced tools.

As companies venture into AI-driven transformations, they must assess their current IT systems and infrastructure to ensure they can accommodate the specific needs of AI technologies, including processing power, storage capacity, and data management requirements. Without an appropriate foundation, even the most skilled teams will struggle to effectively deploy and scale AI initiatives.

One of the first steps in this journey is evaluating the organization's readiness for AI integration. This involves conducting a comprehensive assessment of the existing technology stack, including hardware, software, and data architecture. Businesses need to ask critical questions such as: Do we have the computational power necessary for training and running complex generative AI models? Is our data architecture structured in a way that allows easy access to high-quality data for AI systems? Are our cybersecurity protocols robust enough to protect sensitive AI-generated content and data?

Moreover, executives must decide whether to build custom AI solutions in-house or leverage third-party platforms. Developing custom AI models can offer businesses more control over the specific needs of their operations, but it often requires significant investment in both time and resources, including access to specialized AI talent.

On the other hand, purchasing third-party platforms or leveraging AI-as-a-Service (AIaaS) solutions can offer quicker deployment with less risk, but may come with trade-offs in terms of flexibility, customization, and integration with existing systems. The decision between building or buying AI solutions requires careful consideration of the organization's specific needs, resources, timeline, and long-term strategy.

A key consideration during this process is ensuring that the selected AI technologies are compatible with existing systems and can scale as the business grows. Generative AI tools, in particular, require powerful computing environments, often relying on cloud-based infrastructure or high-performance computing systems to deliver real-time results.

Businesses need to ensure that their current IT infrastructure can support the increased demand for processing power, memory, and storage, especially as AI models become more sophisticated and handle larger datasets.

Additionally, successful integration of AI technologies into business processes requires a focus on long-term scalability. AI is not a one-time implementation; it is an ongoing journey that evolves as new capabilities and technologies emerge. As organizations grow, their AI systems must be able to scale in parallel.

This requires building flexible, modular infrastructure that can accommodate new data sources, integrate with emerging AI tools, and scale as the volume and complexity of tasks increase.

The integration of AI also involves addressing potential challenges related to data management, interoperability between systems, and continuous monitoring of AI performance. AI systems require high-quality, well-structured data to perform effectively.

Therefore, businesses must ensure they have strong data governance frameworks in place, enabling them to manage, clean, and validate data that feeds into AI models.

Furthermore, AI systems must be integrated seamlessly with other business tools and platforms, such as CRM systems, marketing automation tools, and customer service software, ensuring that AI outputs can be easily incorporated into daily operations.

4.1 Assessing Current IT Capabilities

Before diving into the adoption of generative AI, it's essential for an organization to take a comprehensive and strategic look at its existing IT infrastructure. AI technologies, particularly generative AI, come with specific demands that traditional systems may struggle to meet. The complexity of these technologies requires not only advanced computational power but also vast amounts of data and highly efficient data processing pipelines. Organizations must ensure that their current systems can handle the scale and performance requirements of AI applications. An accurate assessment of IT capabilities is the first step in determining whether existing infrastructure will support AI initiatives, or if new investments and upgrades are required.

4.1.1 Evaluating Data Infrastructure

At the heart of any AI-driven initiative is data. Generative AI models are highly dependent on data—both in terms of quality and quantity. For AI to be effective, it needs structured, high-quality data that can be processed efficiently.

As a result, organizations should start by evaluating their current data infrastructure to determine whether it is sufficient to support AI systems. The first point of evaluation is the **quality** of the data. Is the data accurate, free from inconsistencies, and relevant to the business goals? Unclean or poorly structured data will not only hinder AI model performance but could also introduce biases into AI outputs.

Next, organizations should consider the **volume** of data. Generative AI models require large datasets for training, often encompassing terabytes or even petabytes of information. If the data is not available in sufficient quantity or is fragmented across different systems, it may delay or compromise AI initiatives.

The **accessibility** of data is another critical factor. AI solutions can only work effectively if they have easy access to the data they need. This requires the data to be centralized in a way that makes it easy to retrieve and integrate across departments. If data is siloed within various business units, it could lead to inefficiencies and bottlenecks in AI processes.

Organizations should also evaluate the **architecture** of their data storage systems, such as data warehouses, lakes, and analytics platforms. For AI to function optimally, these systems must be designed to handle the high throughput of data required for real-time analysis and model training.

Data must not only be stored securely but also be structured in a way that allows it to be quickly queried, processed, and delivered to AI models. Additionally, it's crucial to have a strong **data management strategy** that ensures data is continuously cleaned, validated, and updated. This is particularly important as AI models rely on the consistency and freshness of data to produce accurate outputs.

Assesing Your Current Data Infraestructure

| Define your data goals & objectives | Map your data sources & data flow | Evaluate your data quality and data governance | Analyze your data integration & data analytics | Benchmark your data performance & data maturity |

4.1.2 Evaluating Computational Power and Cloud Readiness

Another fundamental aspect of assessing current IT capabilities is evaluating whether the organization has the necessary **computational power** to run generative AI models effectively.

Generative AI, particularly large models like GPT-3 or similar deep learning models, requires immense computational resources. These models need **high-performance processors**, such as Graphics Processing Units (GPUs) or Tensor Processing Units (TPUs), which are optimized for the massive parallel processing required by AI algorithms. In addition, these models require significant **memory** and **storage** systems to handle large datasets and store intermediate results during model training and inference.

Traditional on-premise hardware often struggles to meet the performance demands of these models. For many organizations, the solution lies in **cloud computing**. Cloud service providers, such as AWS, Google Cloud, and Microsoft Azure, offer scalable and flexible solutions tailored to meet the computational needs of AI applications. If an organization's infrastructure is not already cloud-based, it is important to evaluate whether a transition to the cloud would be both feasible and beneficial for AI adoption.

Transitioning to the cloud offers several advantages, such as scalable storage and computing power, high availability, and the ability to easily access specialized AI services, such as pre-trained models and machine learning frameworks.

However, moving to the cloud is not a one-size-fits-all solution. Organizations must carefully assess which **cloud platform** aligns best with their existing IT stack, business needs, and security requirements. For example, certain organizations may have already adopted **hybrid cloud** or **multi-cloud** architectures, which can impact the integration of AI solutions. It's important to ensure that cloud services can integrate with the organization's existing tech stack and that the cloud infrastructure supports the desired AI workloads, with an emphasis on security, compliance, and data privacy.

4.1.3 Assessing System Interoperability

AI adoption does not exist in a vacuum. For it to truly benefit the organization, it must be integrated into existing systems and workflows. A critical component of the AI adoption process is assessing the **interoperability** of the organization's existing systems with new AI technologies. This means evaluating whether AI tools can seamlessly integrate with the organization's enterprise systems, such as **Enterprise Resource Planning (ERP), Customer Relationship Management (CRM), supply chain management platforms**, and other critical business applications.

The ability to integrate AI into these systems will determine how effectively AI can automate workflows, analyze data, and provide actionable insights. If the current systems are rigid, outdated, or lack flexibility, the integration of AI could lead to significant inefficiencies and disrupt business processes.

Additionally, poorly integrated systems could lead to the creation of **data silos**, making it more difficult to ensure that AI models have access to the full range of data they need to perform effectively. This lack of seamless integration could also hinder cross-departmental collaboration and result in missed opportunities to leverage AI across the business.

Therefore, assessing system interoperability involves not just evaluating the technical compatibility of new AI tools with existing platforms, but also identifying potential gaps in workflows that might need to be addressed for AI to be implemented effectively. **API integrations, data-sharing**

protocols, and **workflow automation tools** are all essential components that will help ensure AI can be embedded across the organization without requiring major system overhauls. By ensuring that AI solutions can be integrated smoothly into current infrastructure, businesses can maximize the value of AI while minimizing disruptions to day-to-day operations.

Assessing current IT capabilities is a critical first step in the process of AI adoption. This assessment should address data infrastructure, computational power, cloud readiness, and system interoperability, and help identify any gaps in the organization's current IT ecosystem that need to be addressed. By thoroughly evaluating the readiness of existing infrastructure to support AI technologies, businesses can ensure a smooth integration of generative AI solutions and position themselves for long-term success.

4.2 Make vs. Buy Decision Frameworks

The decision between building a custom AI solution in-house (make) or purchasing a pre-built solution from external vendors (buy) is a pivotal one in the process of AI adoption.

This decision is influenced by several factors, including the complexity of the business problem, available resources, time-to-market considerations, and long-term scalability needs. A thorough analysis of these factors is essential for organizations to choose the most effective path that aligns with their strategic goals.

4.2.1 Build (Make): Custom AI Solutions

Building custom AI solutions in-house allows an organization to develop a highly tailored technology that fits precisely with its business needs. This approach gives the organization a high degree of control over the AI models and systems, ensuring that the solutions are closely aligned with proprietary processes, industry-specific requirements, and unique business challenges.

Custom solutions can also provide a competitive advantage by incorporating proprietary algorithms, which can differentiate the company from competitors.

However, building AI solutions in-house requires significant investment in both time and resources. The complexity of AI development means that companies need specialized technical talent such as data scientists, machine learning engineers, AI researchers, and software developers with deep expertise.

In addition, AI projects often have long development cycles that require iterative testing and refinement to ensure the final product meets the required standards.

This approach also requires robust data infrastructure, secure data storage systems, and scalable computational power, all of which demand financial and operational investment.

For businesses with complex or highly specific needs—such as those in specialized industries or those aiming for groundbreaking AI innovation—building a custom AI solution may be the only viable option. It allows for maximum flexibility and control, which can result in long-term strategic benefits, even though it may take longer to develop and implement.

When to Build:

- **High Degree of Customization Required**: If your organization's AI needs are highly specific or unique, building a custom solution ensures that the technology aligns precisely with your business requirements.

- **Proprietary Business Processes**: If your business operates on proprietary processes or needs bespoke solutions to stay ahead of competitors, a custom-built AI solution may be necessary to maintain a competitive edge.

- **Sufficient Technical Expertise**: If your organization has an in-house team of skilled data scientists, engineers, and AI researchers, building a custom solution could be an efficient way to leverage this expertise.

- **Long-Term Competitive Advantage**: When the project is expected to yield a significant, long-term competitive advantage or industry leadership, the resource-intensive nature of custom development may be justified.

4.2.2 Buy (Buy): Pre-Built AI Solutions

Buying pre-built AI solutions offers several advantages, particularly when speed and cost are important considerations. Established technology vendors provide a wide range of AI platforms, from natural language processing (NLP) and image recognition to automation and predictive analytics. These platforms are ready for use out of the box and can be quickly adapted to meet your business's needs. Because these solutions are standardized, they offer a much faster time-to-market compared to building a custom solution from scratch, which can be highly beneficial for organizations looking to implement AI in the short term.

The primary downside of purchasing pre-built solutions is that they are typically less customizable than in-house solutions. While vendors often offer a degree of configurability, these platforms are designed to serve a broad range of industries and use cases. This means that they may not be fully aligned with the unique requirements or workflows of your business.

Additionally, there may be dependency on the vendor for ongoing maintenance, updates, and enhancements, which could limit your control over the solution. However, for organizations that lack the internal resources or technical expertise to develop AI solutions themselves, buying pre-built solutions can be an efficient and cost-effective choice.

Pre-built solutions are especially beneficial when the use case is more standard or has already been addressed by established AI technologies. For example, if the AI application involves simple tasks such as customer segmentation, predictive analytics, or chatbot automation, off-the-shelf products can be deployed quickly and at a lower cost.

When to Buy:

- **Standard Use Cases**: If your use case is a common AI application that is well-supported by existing AI products, buying a pre-built solution can save time and resources.

- **Critical Time-to-Market Needs**: When speed is essential and you need to implement an AI solution rapidly, pre-built platforms can provide a much faster route to deployment than custom-built solutions.

- **Limited Internal Expertise or Resources**: If your organization lacks the specialized in-house talent or infrastructure to develop AI solutions, purchasing a pre-built solution is often the best option.

- **Cost-Effective Solutions**: For businesses looking for straightforward AI applications with minimal customization, buying pre-built solutions provides a budget-friendly option without the overhead of custom development.

4.2.3 Hybrid Approach: Combining Make and Buy

In many cases, a hybrid approach that combines both "make" and "buy" strategies may provide the best of both worlds. This approach involves purchasing pre-built AI platforms for foundational AI functionalities and then customizing them with in-house development to meet specific business needs.

For example, an organization might buy a pre-built platform for basic AI-driven customer support (e.g., a chatbot or helpdesk automation) but then build custom solutions for more advanced, specialized processes like product recommendation engines or complex fraud detection systems.

A hybrid approach allows organizations to leverage the **speed and cost efficiency** of pre-built solutions while still retaining the **flexibility** and **customization** that come with in-house development.

This can be especially beneficial for large organizations or those in dynamic industries where both standard and unique AI applications are required. The hybrid model also provides scalability, as the organization can begin with a solid, ready-made AI foundation and then expand or adapt the solution as its needs evolve.

This approach reduces the risk of starting from scratch while still giving organizations the ability to innovate and differentiate their offerings. By using pre-built platforms to handle standard tasks and custom-built AI for more specialized requirements, companies can maximize the benefits of both strategies.

When to Use a Hybrid Approach:

- **Combination of Standard and Custom Use Cases**: If your organization has both common and unique AI needs, the hybrid approach enables a balance between ready-made solutions and customized development.

- **Scalability and Flexibility**: When you need the flexibility to expand or adjust the AI solution as the business grows, a hybrid approach allows for easy adjustments and expansions without compromising on functionality.

- **Resource Optimization**: Organizations with limited resources may find the hybrid model efficient, as it allows them to handle standard AI applications quickly and focus their in-house talent on solving more complex, high-value problems.

Taking everything into consideration, the **make vs. buy** decision is a critical one for AI adoption. It requires a careful analysis of the organization's technical capabilities, business needs, resource availability, and strategic goals. Building custom AI solutions provides greater control and customization but requires significant investment, time, and expertise.

On the other hand, buying pre-built solutions offers speed, cost-efficiency, and ease of implementation but may lack the flexibility needed for specialized applications. A hybrid approach combines the best of both worlds, enabling organizations to leverage off-the-shelf solutions for standard needs while building customized solutions for unique business challenges.

4.3 Selecting the Right AI Technologies and Partners

Once an organization has made the crucial decision of whether to build or buy its AI solutions, the next step is to carefully select the appropriate AI technologies and partners that will support and drive the business's transformation. This decision is not just about choosing the most advanced AI tools; it's about finding the right fit for your organization's specific goals, needs, and existing infrastructure.

4.3.1 Evaluating AI Technologies

The selection of the right AI technologies is a pivotal factor in ensuring the success of an AI strategy. Since not all AI platforms are built the same, it's crucial to evaluate technologies based on how well they meet your specific business requirements.

A careful and comprehensive evaluation ensures that the organization does not invest in a solution that may later prove incompatible, ineffective, or difficult to scale. Key factors to consider when evaluating AI technologies include:

- **Compatibility**: One of the first things to assess when selecting AI technologies is compatibility with your existing IT infrastructure. AI platforms and tools must integrate smoothly with your current software systems, databases, and tools across the organization. For instance, if you are already using a specific data warehouse solution or CRM system, the AI technology should either integrate directly with these or offer seamless integration options. Compatibility ensures that the AI technology will work harmoniously with the rest of your tech stack and not create roadblocks or require excessive changes to your existing systems.

- **Scalability**: AI models, especially generative models or deep learning networks, require significant computational resources. As AI implementations grow and the business scales, it's critical that the technology can handle increased demand, both in terms of data volume and processing power. When evaluating AI technologies, ensure that they are designed to scale efficiently as your organization's needs expand. Scalable AI solutions allow businesses to continue evolving their AI initiatives without having to completely overhaul their technology as the organization grows.

- **Flexibility**: Business needs, as well as the field of AI itself, evolve rapidly. Therefore, the AI technology selected should be flexible enough to adapt to changing business requirements, new trends in AI, and advancements in algorithms or machine learning techniques. Look for platforms that offer modularity, allowing you to add or adjust features over time without having to completely redesign the AI solution. Flexibility also means that the technology can accommodate new data sources, changing workflows, or updated regulatory requirements, making it an essential quality for long-term viability.

- **Performance**: Evaluating the performance of AI technologies is critical to ensuring that they meet business goals and deliver measurable value. Assess the capabilities of the AI tools through case studies, benchmarks, and customer testimonials. Understanding how the technology has performed in real-world applications can provide insight into its ability to handle your specific business needs. Also, look for performance metrics such as processing speed, accuracy, and reliability to ensure the technology can deliver the outcomes your business expects.

4.3.2 Choosing AI Partners

Whether you choose to build or buy AI solutions, selecting the right AI partners is essential to the success of your strategy. AI is a complex, rapidly evolving field, and partnering with the right organizations can help mitigate risks and accelerate progress.

AI partners can provide more than just technology—they can offer expertise, insights, and resources that can significantly enhance the quality and speed of your AI implementation.

- **In-house Development**: If you decide to build AI solutions internally, AI consulting firms, technology service providers, and specialized development agencies can help guide the development process. These partners can offer valuable technical expertise, help with the design and implementation of AI models, and even assist in hiring or training specialized talent. AI consulting firms bring industry-specific experience and can provide insights on best practices, as well as help manage risks associated with AI adoption.

- **Purchasing AI Solutions**: If you opt to buy pre-built AI solutions, the vendor selection becomes a key part of your success. Choose partners who have a proven track record of successful AI implementations, a deep understanding of the industry, and a commitment to innovation and continuous support. Your chosen vendor should be capable of offering AI platforms that not only meet current business requirements but are also flexible enough to adapt to future needs. Industry giants like IBM Watson, Google Cloud AI, and Microsoft Azure AI offer reliable, scalable platforms, but smaller, specialized vendors may provide niche solutions that are better suited to your specific needs.

4.3.3 Vendor Evaluation Criteria

When evaluating potential AI vendors, there are several criteria that should guide your decision-making process. This ensures that the vendor chosen can meet your long-term needs and provide ongoing value to the organization.

- **Reputation and Track Record**: A strong reputation and a proven track record in deploying AI solutions successfully are essential when selecting an AI partner. Look for vendors with a history of delivering tangible results across industries that are similar to yours. A vendor's ability to showcase successful implementations with measurable outcomes, such as efficiency improvements, cost savings, or innovation, provides confidence that they can deliver on your needs. Asking for references or reviewing case studies can help assess the vendor's experience.

- **Support and Training**: The chosen AI technology should come with comprehensive support and training resources. Ensure that the vendor offers adequate resources, such as tutorials, documentation, and dedicated customer service teams, to assist your team in effectively implementing and utilizing the solution. Additionally, evaluate the vendor's willingness to provide ongoing training, helping your employees understand how to use the system to its fullest potential. Strong vendor support can significantly reduce the complexity of AI adoption, especially if your team lacks prior experience with the technology.

- **Security and Compliance**: Security is a paramount concern when working with AI solutions, particularly those that process sensitive or personal data. When evaluating vendors, ensure that the AI platform complies with industry-specific regulations, such as GDPR for data privacy, HIPAA for healthcare, or any other relevant local or international data protection laws. The vendor should be able to provide certifications, detailed security protocols, and a clear understanding of how their AI technology protects against potential data breaches or misuse.

- **Cost and ROI**: While the cost should not be the sole determining factor, it is essential to ensure that the AI solution provides a clear return on investment (ROI). Take into account not only the initial purchase or development costs but also ongoing maintenance, training, and support fees. Evaluate the potential indirect benefits, such as efficiency improvements, time savings, and competitive advantages, that will come from deploying the AI solution. A solid ROI calculation helps ensure that the investment in AI technology aligns with your company's long-term business objectives.

4.3.4 Strategic Considerations for Partnering in AI

In addition to the technical and operational factors discussed, strategic considerations must also play a role in your vendor and partner selection process. Partnerships with AI providers or consultants should align with your broader business objectives and transformation goals.

Look for vendors who share your vision for AI and are willing to collaborate on future developments and refinements. Long-term partnerships with vendors that offer continuous innovation and updates can ensure that your AI solutions remain cutting-edge as the field evolves. The right AI partner will act as a trusted advisor, not just a technology supplier, offering insights, advice, and expertise that help drive business growth and digital transformation.

By carefully evaluating both the technologies and the partners that will support your AI initiatives, your organization can ensure that it is well-positioned to successfully implement and leverage AI for competitive advantage, efficiency, and innovation.

4.4 Ensuring Scalability and Compatibility

Scalability and compatibility are two of the most critical considerations when implementing AI technologies within an organization. As businesses grow and as AI models become more sophisticated, the infrastructure that supports these technologies must evolve accordingly.

Ensuring that AI systems can scale without causing disruption to ongoing operations is essential for maintaining business continuity and realizing the full potential of AI. Additionally, the ability of AI systems to integrate smoothly with existing technology infrastructure is vital to maximizing efficiency and minimizing the risk of data silos or workflow disruptions.

4.4.1 Cloud-Based Solutions for Scalability

One of the most effective ways to achieve scalability in AI deployment is by leveraging cloud-based platforms. Cloud solutions offer businesses the flexibility to scale resources up or down depending on the specific demands of AI models.

As AI models become more complex and as the volume of data increases, cloud platforms provide on-demand access to virtually unlimited computational resources. This scalability allows organizations to handle the increasing demands of AI without the need for significant upfront investments in physical infrastructure.

In addition to flexibility, cloud platforms provide access to cutting-edge technologies and infrastructure, including powerful GPUs and TPUs necessary for training advanced AI models. Cloud providers, such as Amazon Web Services (AWS), Microsoft Azure, and Google Cloud, offer specialized services and tools designed to support AI workloads.

These platforms also handle maintenance, security updates, and performance optimization, reducing the burden on internal IT teams. Cloud solutions also eliminate the need for businesses to worry about hardware obsolescence, as these platforms continually upgrade their systems to keep pace with technological advancements.

Furthermore, cloud-based solutions offer businesses the agility to quickly adapt to changing market conditions or business needs. If an organization needs to process larger volumes of data, deploy new AI models, or scale operations rapidly, the cloud can accommodate these needs with minimal disruption, allowing businesses to stay ahead of competitors and reduce time-to-market for AI-driven innovations.

4.4.2 Modular Architecture

Another key factor in ensuring the long-term scalability and flexibility of AI systems is adopting a modular architecture. Modular AI solutions allow businesses to add new features or scale their systems incrementally, rather than requiring a complete overhaul of the existing infrastructure. This approach minimizes the risk of disruption to day-to-day operations and ensures that the organization can continuously evolve its AI capabilities without starting from scratch.

Modular architectures are especially beneficial for organizations looking to implement AI in stages. Rather than attempting to deploy a comprehensive AI solution all at once, businesses can start with a basic model or platform and then expand as their needs grow or as new AI technologies become available. This incremental approach allows for smoother transitions and enables the organization to address specific business challenges without the need for a full-scale implementation upfront.

Additionally, modularity ensures that the AI systems remain adaptable to future technological advancements. As AI methodologies evolve or new tools emerge, businesses can simply integrate these new components into their existing architecture without having to replace their entire infrastructure. This flexibility is crucial in a rapidly changing field like AI, where new breakthroughs and innovations are continually reshaping the landscape.

4.4.3 Ensuring Integration with Legacy Systems

A major consideration when adopting AI is the ability of new AI systems to integrate seamlessly with an organization's legacy systems. Many companies already rely on a range of established technologies, such as Enterprise Resource Planning (ERP) systems, Customer Relationship Management (CRM) tools, and business intelligence platforms. These legacy systems often contain critical data and workflows that need to be incorporated into AI initiatives to ensure continuity and accuracy.

It is essential that the AI solutions adopted do not require completely replacing or discarding these existing systems. Instead, AI technology should be able to integrate effectively with legacy tools, allowing for a smooth flow of data across the organization. Ensuring integration helps avoid data silos, which can undermine the effectiveness of AI models. AI-powered insights should be able to inform and enhance existing workflows, not disrupt them.

Using APIs (Application Programming Interfaces) or middleware solutions is a common way to facilitate this integration. APIs enable different systems to communicate with one another, allowing AI platforms to access data from ERP or CRM systems, for instance, without requiring significant changes to those systems themselves. Middleware solutions can also serve as intermediaries, ensuring compatibility between different technologies and facilitating the transfer of data across systems.

Additionally, the use of integration frameworks and standards can help streamline the process of connecting AI systems with legacy software. These solutions ensure that data is consistent, accurate, and easily accessible for AI models, which is critical for achieving reliable results. With proper integration, AI can enhance existing business processes by offering new insights, improving automation, and driving efficiencies without the need for complete system overhauls.

In conclusion, ensuring the scalability and compatibility of AI technologies within an organization is critical for long-term success. By leveraging cloud-based solutions, adopting modular architectures, and ensuring seamless integration with legacy systems, businesses can implement AI in a way that is both efficient and sustainable.

This approach allows organizations to grow their AI capabilities over time, ensuring that their technology infrastructure remains capable of supporting more complex AI models and larger datasets as the business expands.

Chapter 5: Implementation and Scaling Strategies

Implementing and scaling generative AI technologies requires more than just selecting the right tools and building the necessary infrastructure. It demands a structured, strategic approach to testing, expanding, and ensuring the long-term success of AI initiatives.

Without a well-thought-out plan, AI projects risk falling short of their full potential. A comprehensive approach starts with launching pilot programs that allow businesses to test AI models on a smaller scale and assess their real-world effectiveness. Successful pilot programs provide insights into potential challenges and necessary adjustments, setting the stage for wider adoption.

From there, the scaling process must be data-driven, ensuring that expansion is both efficient and aligned with strategic goals. Real-time metrics and feedback loops play a critical role in guiding this process, helping organizations optimize their AI solutions and make informed decisions on further investment.

Ultimately, a structured approach, supported by best practices and continuous monitoring, helps ensure that AI initiatives are not only successfully implemented but also scale sustainably over time. Real-world case studies can provide additional guidance on how other organizations have navigated this journey, offering valuable lessons on how to achieve success with AI at scale.

5.1 Pilot Program Design

The first step in integrating generative AI into your organization is designing a pilot program. This allows you to test the technology in a controlled environment, validate its effectiveness, and identify any potential challenges before rolling it out organization-wide. A well-designed pilot can also help build internal support and generate early buy-in from stakeholders.

By offering a proof of concept in a low-risk setting, it provides a tangible demonstration of AI's value, ensuring stakeholders have confidence in its future success. Additionally, a pilot program enables organizations to identify potential gaps in their understanding or resources, which can be addressed early in the process, minimizing disruption when scaling AI solutions across the entire business.

5.1.1 Defining the Pilot Scope and Objectives

Start by clearly defining the scope of your pilot program. Which specific business problems or use cases are you trying to solve with AI? What key metrics or outcomes will define success? By narrowing the focus, you ensure that the pilot is manageable and measurable, setting realistic expectations for what the AI solution can achieve in its initial phase. It's important to frame the objectives in a way that reflects not only the technical capabilities of the AI but also the strategic goals of the organization.

For example, if the pilot aims to improve customer support efficiency using an AI-driven chatbot, the objectives might include reducing response times, increasing customer satisfaction, or improving first-call resolution rates. Clear, data-driven objectives provide a way to track progress and ensure that the AI solution is delivering the expected value.

The objectives should be specific and aligned with your organization's strategic goals. For instance, if the company's primary concern is enhancing operational efficiency, then the pilot should be designed to test how the AI can reduce resource consumption, automate workflows, or improve output quality.

Moreover, the pilot's metrics should not only be quantitative but also qualitative, addressing how AI impacts user experience, employee engagement, or overall business agility. Defining success metrics upfront ensures that you can objectively evaluate the pilot's results. This alignment with business goals also increases the likelihood that the pilot will receive ongoing support and resources throughout its implementation.

5.1.2 Choosing the Right Use Cases for Pilot Testing

Not every AI initiative needs to be tested through a pilot program. It's important to choose use cases that will deliver measurable results quickly and provide insights into the broader potential of AI for your business. Ideal use cases for pilots are typically those that:

- Are aligned with key business priorities.

- Have clear, measurable outcomes.

- Have a manageable level of complexity and risk.

- Are likely to deliver visible benefits in a short timeframe.

The pilot should focus on areas where AI can demonstrate a tangible impact in a relatively short time. For example, a pilot that uses generative AI for content creation in marketing might be a good fit if the business wants to test AI's ability to scale content production, streamline workflows, and enhance creative outputs without sacrificing quality.

Similarly, piloting AI in customer service could demonstrate its ability to automate routine queries, improving response times, reducing operational costs, and freeing up human agents for more complex tasks. The use case should be designed so that the AI's impact is clear and easily measurable.

Another important consideration when choosing use cases is ensuring that the pilot aligns with business objectives and provides insights into how AI could be scaled across the organization.

For example, an AI tool designed to streamline supply chain processes or optimize inventory management could be tested in a small but impactful segment, such as a single product line or warehouse, before broader adoption. This approach helps uncover potential challenges while still providing immediate value, ensuring that the broader AI implementation is based on real-world insights and not just theoretical projections.

5.1.3 Stakeholder Engagement and Communication

Successful pilots require strong stakeholder engagement. Involve key decision-makers and business leaders early in the design process to secure buy-in and ensure alignment with business goals. Engaging stakeholders from the outset helps identify potential roadblocks and ensures that the project receives the necessary support and resources. It also ensures that the pilot is structured to address the key concerns and pain points that leaders care about, helping to secure their commitment to AI initiatives beyond the pilot phase.

Effective communication is also critical to managing expectations. Be transparent about the pilot's scope, timeline, and expected outcomes. Managing expectations up front helps mitigate frustration in case the pilot doesn't achieve all of its goals or encounters unforeseen challenges.

Make sure all participants understand the goals, their roles, and how they contribute to the success of the project. A comprehensive communication strategy ensures that everyone involved is on the same page and motivated to contribute to the pilot's success.

Additionally, clearly outline the anticipated benefits and any risks, such as potential disruptions during the testing phase.

Open and transparent communication throughout the pilot will increase trust and reduce resistance, especially when results might not immediately meet expectations. Being upfront about potential risks and providing regular updates on progress helps keep stakeholders engaged and supportive of the initiative. Furthermore, clear communication fosters a culture of accountability, where team members take ownership of their tasks and feel empowered to make adjustments as needed during the pilot phase.

By strategically designing the pilot program, selecting the right use cases, and engaging stakeholders, businesses can set a solid foundation for successful AI adoption.

5.2 Metrics-Driven Expansion

Once your pilot program has been successfully tested, the next phase is scaling up. To do this effectively, you must rely on data-driven insights to inform your scaling decisions. The key to expanding AI capabilities across the organization is developing a metrics-driven approach, which ensures that every step of the expansion is justified, measurable, and aligned with strategic goals.

By using objective, quantifiable data to guide your decisions, you minimize risks associated with scaling and ensure that your AI initiatives deliver consistent value. This approach not only helps track the performance of AI but also allows for continuous optimization as the technology is integrated across the organization.

5.2.1 Key Performance Indicators (KPIs) for Scaling AI

Establishing KPIs that reflect the success of your AI initiative is vital for tracking progress and justifying broader implementation. KPIs should be aligned with business objectives, providing clear benchmarks that enable you to assess AI's impact and determine its scalability. These KPIs will serve as the foundation for making data-driven decisions, ensuring that AI investments are directly tied to organizational outcomes. Possible KPIs for scaling AI could include:

- **Cost Reduction**: Is the AI solution helping to reduce operational costs? For instance, AI-powered automation in customer support can help reduce the need for human agents, thus lowering staffing costs. Additionally, AI can help streamline procurement, reduce waste, and identify inefficiencies that result in cost savings across the organization.

- **Efficiency Gains**: Is the AI system improving operational efficiency or speeding up decision-making processes? In areas such as logistics or supply chain management, AI can optimize routes, inventory management, or demand forecasting, leading to faster decision-making and resource allocation. The more AI streamlines operations, the more it can scale to other departments with similar efficiencies.

- **Customer Satisfaction**: Has AI improved customer satisfaction metrics such as Net Promoter Score (NPS) or Customer Satisfaction Score (CSAT)? If AI is deployed in customer-facing roles—such as chatbots or recommendation engines—tracking these metrics will show how well AI meets customer expectations. Improvements in customer satisfaction are often the most direct measure of AI's value in business operations.

- **Revenue Growth**: Has the AI initiative contributed to increased sales, higher conversion rates, or new revenue streams? For example, personalized marketing powered by AI can increase customer engagement, leading to higher conversion rates and, ultimately, more sales. This could also include AI's role in developing new business models, enhancing product offerings, or creating new market opportunities.

- **Employee Productivity**: Has AI improved employee productivity by automating repetitive tasks or augmenting their decision-making capabilities? By measuring productivity gains, you can assess whether AI is freeing up employees to focus on higher-value activities, which can directly influence business outcomes.

5.2.2 Data-Driven Decision Making

To scale AI effectively, use data-driven decision-making at every stage of the process. Collect detailed feedback from the pilot program, analyze performance against the defined KPIs, and make adjustments as necessary.

This approach ensures that scaling decisions are informed by evidence, helping to identify areas where AI is most effective and ensuring that resources are allocated wisely. Collecting and analyzing data is also essential in refining the AI model, improving its accuracy, and addressing any unforeseen challenges before they become widespread issues.

The feedback loop should involve continuous monitoring, tracking, and refining of AI systems to ensure that the scaling process is both effective and efficient. For instance, if the data shows that a particular AI solution is underperforming in certain areas, you can make adjustments in real time rather than waiting for issues to compound as you scale. An iterative approach ensures the AI solution evolves in response to real-world performance, allowing for greater optimization as the system expands.

Analyzing the data can also help identify areas for improvement and determine whether further testing or refinements are needed. Regular reviews of performance metrics will ensure that scaling is done in a controlled, efficient manner, without overextending resources or making overly ambitious commitments. Data-driven decisions also allow for a more agile approach to scaling, where adjustments can be made quickly based on performance outcomes, market changes, or shifting organizational priorities.

5.2.3 Scaling Based on Success

After validating the pilot program's success through KPI analysis, the next step is to begin expanding AI use in phases. This phased approach reduces risks and allows teams to fine-tune the technology as it is implemented across different departments. Rather than a full-scale rollout, this gradual expansion ensures that each phase of scaling is based on real success stories and lessons learned from the initial pilot. By starting small and progressively broadening the AI solution, organizations can learn from early deployments, correct any issues, and ensure the technology is effectively integrated into the organization before it becomes pervasive.

For example, if the AI-powered marketing campaign in your pilot generated high engagement and increased conversions, the next step might involve expanding AI-driven personalization to other customer touchpoints, such as email campaigns, social media interactions, or product recommendations.

This incremental approach reduces the risk of major disruptions and ensures the solution is working effectively in different contexts. Similarly, AI could be gradually integrated into other business functions—such as human resources, finance, or operations—based on the outcomes and insights from the initial pilot phase. By scaling based on validated success, organizations can ensure AI is deployed in the areas where it delivers the most impact, making the expansion process smoother and more successful overall.

This approach allows for better management of organizational change. Scaling AI is not just about implementing new technologies, but also about transforming business processes, culture, and workflows. Each phase of scaling should involve the necessary training, upskilling, and change management to ensure the workforce is ready to embrace AI and leverage its capabilities effectively.

5.3 Best Practices for Successful Rollout

To ensure that your AI solution scales successfully and delivers the expected results, it's essential to adopt best practices that guide a seamless and effective rollout. The process of integrating AI into your organization is a transformative journey that requires careful planning, strategic execution, and constant refinement. By following these best practices, you can avoid common pitfalls and maximize the potential of your AI initiatives.

5.3.1 Start Small, Scale Gradually

One of the most critical pieces of advice when rolling out AI technology is to start small and scale gradually. While the allure of quickly implementing AI at full scale is tempting, it's important to recognize that large-scale deployments carry inherent risks, including unforeseen technical issues, resistance from employees, and possible disruptions to business operations. By starting with smaller, focused pilot projects, organizations can test the technology in a more controlled environment, reducing the chances of significant disruptions.

The initial rollout should aim to address a specific, well-defined use case with measurable outcomes. Once the solution proves successful in this initial phase, you can expand incrementally, building on lessons learned and refining the system. This gradual approach not only minimizes risk but also helps in building internal confidence and fostering adoption, as teams will have time to adapt to the technology and witness its tangible benefits. Scaling in phases also provides flexibility—if any problems arise, it's easier to address them in smaller, localized contexts without impacting the broader organization.

5.3.2 Cross-Functional Collaboration

AI implementation should not be siloed within a single department or team. For the solution to be successful and provide maximum value, it's vital to encourage cross-functional collaboration across multiple departments. AI adoption requires the expertise of various stakeholders, including IT, data science, operations, marketing, and customer service. Each department plays a crucial role in ensuring that AI is integrated effectively into their operations and is aligned with the specific goals of the organization.

Collaboration between teams fosters a holistic understanding of AI's potential and ensures that the technology is tailored to meet the diverse needs of the business.

For instance, while the marketing department may use AI for customer segmentation, personalized campaigns, and targeting, the sales department may focus on AI for lead scoring, sales forecasting, and automation of routine tasks. By involving all relevant departments, organizations ensure that AI isn't implemented as a one-size-fits-all solution but is fine-tuned for each department's unique challenges and opportunities.

Furthermore, cross-functional collaboration helps identify potential gaps and synergies where AI can be deployed to drive more value. For example, insights gained from customer service could inform product development teams on recurring issues, while data from the sales team could help enhance the AI's predictive capabilities. Regular communication between departments will ensure that AI systems evolve based on real-time feedback from the business and users, creating a more integrated and effective AI ecosystem.

5.3.3 Continuous Monitoring and Feedback

Even after an AI solution has been successfully scaled, its effectiveness should not be assumed to be static. Continuous monitoring and feedback loops are essential to ensuring that the AI system remains relevant, functional, and aligned with the organization's evolving needs.

Just as AI models require ongoing training and refinement, the deployment process requires continuous evaluation to optimize performance and outcomes.

Monitoring the AI system should include tracking key performance indicators (KPIs) established during the pilot phase. However, it's not enough to simply track metrics such as cost reduction, efficiency gains, or customer satisfaction; organizations must also monitor user adoption and employee engagement.

This ensures that the AI tools are not only effective but also embraced by the teams who are expected to use them. Regular performance reviews help identify areas of improvement, allowing adjustments to be made proactively rather than reactively.

In addition to internal monitoring, gathering feedback from both employees and customers is crucial for refining AI systems. End-users, including employees interacting with AI tools and customers engaging with AI-driven products or services, are in the best position to provide valuable insights into how well the system is meeting their needs.

Establishing a culture of feedback, where users feel comfortable providing input, can highlight friction points or new opportunities for improvement. Feedback loops ensure that AI remains agile, adapting to changing market conditions, user expectations, and emerging technological advancements.

By maintaining a constant cycle of monitoring and feedback, organizations can continue to fine-tune AI systems, ensuring their longevity and maximizing their impact across the business. Additionally, this iterative approach allows for better risk management, as any emerging issues can be addressed before they escalate into larger problems, ensuring that AI remains a trusted, high-performing asset for the organization.

The successful rollout of AI is not a one-time event, but a continuous journey that requires careful planning, collaboration, and ongoing evaluation. By starting small, fostering cross-functional collaboration, and maintaining a focus on continuous monitoring and feedback, organizations can ensure that their AI initiatives scale successfully and provide lasting value.

5.4 Case Studies of Effective Implementation

5.4.1 Case Study: AI in Customer Service at a Telecom Provider

A leading telecom provider sought to enhance its customer service operations and reduce the strain on its call center by implementing an AI-powered chatbot. This chatbot was designed to handle a wide range of basic customer inquiries, such as billing questions, service outages, and account management. Initially, the telecom company launched a small pilot program in a single region, with the primary metrics for success being customer satisfaction, response times, and call volume reduction.

The pilot proved to be an outstanding success. The chatbot effectively handled approximately 30% of the call center's incoming inquiries, which resulted in a significant 30% reduction in call volume. This decrease in call volume allowed human agents to focus on more complex issues, leading to a 15% improvement in overall customer satisfaction. Additionally, operational costs were reduced by 20%, primarily due to the reduction in the need for live agents and the improved efficiency of the AI system.

Following the positive results of the pilot, the telecom provider expanded the chatbot to additional regions, and soon, the AI-powered solution was integrated across all customer service functions, including troubleshooting and technical support. This phased rollout allowed the company to monitor performance closely and adjust as necessary, ultimately demonstrating that AI could be effectively scaled across a large organization. The company's successful implementation showcased the tangible benefits of AI in improving operational efficiency, customer experience, and cost management.

5.4.2 Case Study: AI-Powered Content Creation in Marketing

A global e-commerce brand sought to automate its content creation and marketing efforts to improve efficiency and scalability. The company turned to an AI-driven content creation platform, which was initially tested for generating product descriptions and social media posts. This pilot project was critical as the brand needed to maintain its unique voice while generating a large volume of content across multiple platforms. The AI solution was designed to write content quickly while adhering to brand guidelines.

The pilot program was a resounding success, producing content 50% faster than manual methods, while also achieving a higher conversion rate on product pages and social media posts. The ability to produce content at scale without sacrificing quality enabled the e-commerce brand to maintain consistency across its marketing channels while saving time. The results of the pilot provided confidence in the AI's capabilities, and the company decided to expand the use of AI-driven content generation to other marketing areas, such as email campaigns, blog posts, and customer engagement activities.

To ensure that quality and the brand's voice were preserved, the company introduced an iterative scaling process. Content produced by the AI system was carefully reviewed by human editors, who made adjustments as necessary to ensure that the final output was aligned with brand guidelines. This gradual scaling process ensured that the expansion of AI tools did not disrupt the overall marketing strategy and allowed the company to continue driving efficiency while maintaining the integrity of its brand messaging.

5.4.3 Case Study: AI in Healthcare Diagnostics

A healthcare provider sought to leverage AI to assist doctors in diagnosing medical conditions more accurately and efficiently. The provider integrated AI-driven diagnostic tools that utilized machine learning algorithms to analyze medical images, such as chest X-rays, for early signs of disease. The initial pilot was implemented in a select group of hospitals, with a focus on using AI to identify potential issues such as pneumonia, tuberculosis, and lung cancer.

The pilot produced impressive results, with the AI tool demonstrating diagnostic accuracy rates comparable to those of expert radiologists. In fact, in many instances, the AI system was able to detect anomalies that were missed by human reviewers, leading to earlier intervention and better outcomes for patients. This success was pivotal for expanding AI use into additional diagnostic areas, such as mammography and brain imaging. As a result, the healthcare provider saw improvements in diagnosis accuracy and a reduction in time to treatment.

The phased expansion of AI tools was implemented cautiously, with each new diagnostic area undergoing extensive validation before being rolled out across the entire network.

This approach ensured that the integration of AI in healthcare was both safe and effective, ultimately enhancing the provider's ability to deliver timely, accurate diagnoses. The integration of AI-driven diagnostics also freed up healthcare professionals to focus on more complex cases, reducing clinician burnout and improving overall healthcare delivery.

These case studies demonstrate that AI, when properly implemented and scaled, can drive significant improvements in operational efficiency, customer satisfaction, and business outcomes.

Whether in customer service, marketing, or healthcare, AI offers powerful solutions that can transform business operations, increase productivity, and enhance decision-making capabilities. Each of these examples also highlights the importance of starting with a well-defined pilot program, gathering data-driven insights, and scaling gradually to ensure long-term success.

Chapter 6: Ethical Governance and Risk Management

As generative AI continues to transform business operations, ensuring that its deployment aligns with ethical standards and mitigates potential risks is paramount.

While AI offers immense opportunities for innovation and efficiency, its integration into business processes must be carefully managed to avoid unintended consequences, such as biases, data breaches, and non-compliance with evolving regulations. Ethical governance and robust risk management are not just compliance requirements but also foundational to building trust with customers, stakeholders, and employees.

This chapter delves into how organizations can establish ethical governance frameworks, address potential risks, and ensure that AI is used responsibly. From tackling AI bias and reliability concerns to safeguarding privacy and complying with regulations, a strong ethical approach is essential for sustainable AI adoption.

6.1 Addressing AI Bias and Reliability Concerns

One of the most significant ethical challenges in AI deployment is the potential for bias. AI systems learn from large datasets, which may contain biases inherent in historical data or the ways in which data is collected. If these biases are not addressed, AI systems can perpetuate and even amplify existing inequalities, leading to unfair outcomes that may harm individuals or entire groups. As AI continues to play a crucial role in decision-making processes across various industries, from hiring to criminal justice, ensuring fairness and reliability becomes a central issue.

The consequences of AI bias can be severe, affecting marginalized communities and reinforcing societal stereotypes, making it a critical area for organizations to focus on as they implement AI technologies.

6.1.1 Identifying and Mitigating Bias

Bias in AI systems can manifest in many different ways. Often, it arises from biased data—data that is unrepresentative or skewed due to historical prejudices or the methods by which data is collected.

For example, if a facial recognition system is predominantly trained on images of light-skinned individuals, it will perform poorly on darker-skinned individuals. In other cases, bias may emerge from poorly designed algorithms or the inadvertent biases introduced during model development by the people involved.

Bias in AI can also stem from social inequalities that are reflected in the data used to train these systems. It is therefore essential for organizations to be proactive in identifying and addressing these biases to avoid perpetuating existing disparities.

To mitigate bias, organizations should take several crucial steps:

- **Use Diverse and Representative Datasets**: Ensure that the data used to train AI models is diverse and representative of the target population. This includes accounting for demographic factors such as age, gender, race, socioeconomic status, and other relevant attributes. Organizations should audit existing datasets to identify any imbalances or underrepresentation of certain groups, which could lead to biased outcomes. For example, ensuring that training data for AI used in hiring processes includes a balanced representation of candidates from different ethnicities, genders, and backgrounds can help mitigate bias in recruitment decisions.

- **Bias Audits and Algorithmic Fairness**: Regular bias audits are essential to ensure that AI systems are not producing discriminatory outcomes. These audits involve evaluating AI models for potential biases and testing the fairness of decisions made by these systems. There are various fairness metrics and algorithms that can be applied during the model training process to promote more equitable outcomes. Techniques like adversarial debiasing or the incorporation of fairness constraints during training can help to adjust the model to reduce bias in predictions. Fairness constraints, for example, can ensure that the model treats different demographic groups equally, regardless of their characteristics.

- **Transparency in AI Decision-Making**: Creating explainable AI (XAI) is crucial for fostering transparency in how AI models arrive at their decisions. This is particularly important in high-stakes domains such as hiring, lending, and healthcare, where biased decisions can have serious social and legal consequences. Explainability allows users to understand why a particular decision was made, helping to identify any unintentional biases. For instance, if an AI system used in hiring disproportionately rejects applicants from certain demographic groups, explainable AI tools can reveal which factors in the data are contributing to these biased outcomes. Transparency also allows for greater accountability and provides users with the opportunity to challenge or appeal AI decisions when they are unfair.

6.1.2 Reliability and Accountability in AI Systems

Reliability and accountability are crucial when deploying AI systems, especially in areas where decisions have a direct impact on people's lives, such as healthcare, finance, or autonomous vehicles. AI systems must be dependable, accurate, and capable of performing consistently under various conditions. This is particularly true for high-risk areas where faulty decision-making could lead to harm, such as in medical diagnostics or self-driving car navigation.

To ensure the reliability of AI systems, organizations should implement the following practices:

- **Robust Testing and Validation**: Before deploying AI systems at scale, organizations should conduct extensive testing and validation in controlled environments to assess the model's performance under different scenarios. This includes evaluating how the AI system behaves under edge cases, where the data is unusual or extreme, as well as stress testing the system to ensure its robustness. For example, an AI-powered diagnostic tool used in healthcare should be tested on a wide range of medical conditions and patient demographics to ensure that it performs well in all situations. Stress testing can also involve simulating unexpected inputs, such as rare diseases or unusual imaging patterns, to determine how the model reacts and whether it can still provide accurate diagnoses.

- **Continuous Monitoring and Feedback Loops**: Even after deployment, AI models require continuous monitoring to ensure their ongoing reliability. This monitoring can help detect any shifts in performance or areas where the model may start producing biased or inaccurate results. Implementing feedback loops is also critical, as they allow organizations to gather data on how the AI system is performing in real-world scenarios. This feedback can then be used to refine and adjust the model over time. For instance, an AI system used for demand forecasting in retail may experience shifts in accuracy during seasonal periods, such as holidays or major sales events, which require recalibration based on new consumer behavior trends.

- **Accountability Mechanisms**: It is essential to establish clear accountability structures for AI decision-making processes. While AI systems are designed to automate decision-making, they must still be overseen by humans who are responsible for ensuring the system operates fairly and reliably. Accountability mechanisms help ensure that there is a clear understanding of who is responsible when AI systems make errors or produce unexpected outcomes. This can include creating a dedicated team to monitor AI decisions, establishing protocols for investigating any issues that arise, and putting in place systems to audit AI models regularly. In healthcare, for example, if an AI tool misidentifies a condition, a human doctor should have the final authority to review and approve the diagnosis before any treatment is administered. This human oversight helps ensure that critical decisions are not solely left to machines.

Addressing AI bias and ensuring reliability are critical components of successful AI deployment. By using diverse datasets, conducting regular audits, promoting transparency, and ensuring robust testing and monitoring, organizations can build AI systems that are not only effective but also fair and trustworthy. This will help mitigate the risks associated with biased or unreliable AI and ensure that the technology benefits everyone, regardless of their background or context.

6.2 Data Privacy and Security Protocols

As AI systems process vast amounts of data, often including personal and sensitive information, ensuring data privacy and security becomes a core element of ethical governance. Mishandling data can result in serious consequences, including reputational damage, legal repercussions, and a significant loss of public trust. In today's data-driven world, consumers are becoming increasingly aware of how their personal information is used, making it imperative for organizations to safeguard that data while respecting privacy rights. When deploying AI technologies, organizations must not only adhere to privacy regulations but also take proactive steps to prevent data breaches and ensure that their systems are secure from cyber threats. Ensuring robust privacy and security protocols within AI systems helps build trust, mitigates the risks associated with data misuse, and protects sensitive information from potential harm.

6.2.1 Ensuring Compliance with Data Privacy Laws

To maintain ethical standards and protect individuals' privacy, AI initiatives must comply with a wide range of data privacy regulations. Some of the most important regulations include the European Union's General Data Protection Regulation (GDPR), the California Consumer Privacy Act (CCPA), and other regional or industry-specific laws. These regulations impose strict requirements on organizations regarding how they collect, store, and process personal data. The following practices should be implemented to ensure compliance:

- **Obtain Explicit Consent**: AI applications that collect personal data must secure informed consent from users. This consent must be specific, granular, and freely given, meaning users are fully aware of what data is being collected, why it is being collected, and how it will be used. The process should also allow users to withdraw their consent at any time, which is a fundamental right under laws like GDPR. For instance, if an AI system is collecting data to train a model for personalized recommendations, the user must be able to opt-in, clearly knowing the type of data being collected and how it will impact their user experience. Additionally, businesses should implement an easy mechanism for users to revoke consent, such as through a user-friendly settings interface.

- **Data Minimization and Purpose Limitation**: Under data protection laws, AI systems should only process the minimum amount of data required to achieve a specific purpose. This principle of data minimization mandates that organizations limit their data collection to what is absolutely necessary for the task at hand. For example, if AI is used to recommend products on an e-commerce website, it should not collect excessive personal data beyond what is required to personalize the recommendations, such as browsing history or past purchases. Furthermore, organizations must clearly articulate the purpose of data collection to users and ensure that the data is not used for purposes beyond the original scope. This helps to ensure that users' data is not exploited for unintended or unnecessary purposes.

- **Right to Access and Erasure**: A core tenet of privacy laws like GDPR is the right of individuals to access their personal data, correct inaccuracies, and request deletion of their data if desired. Organizations must design AI systems in a way that allows users to easily exercise these rights. For example, a user who feels their data is being improperly processed or stored should have the ability to access their data, request corrections, or even ask for their data to be deleted. Incorporating these features into the design of AI systems is not only required by law but is also crucial for fostering trust with consumers. Businesses must establish processes to respond to access requests within the legal timeframes and ensure data deletion is handled in compliance with the regulations.

6.2.2 Implementing Strong Data Security Measures

With the increasing use of AI comes an elevated risk of data breaches and malicious attacks. To mitigate these risks, organizations must implement comprehensive data security measures that safeguard sensitive personal information throughout its lifecycle—from collection and storage to transmission and processing. The following best practices can help enhance data security:

- **Encryption and Anonymization**: Sensitive data should always be encrypted both at rest and in transit to prevent unauthorized access. Encryption transforms the data into a format that cannot be read without the proper decryption key, making it difficult for cybercriminals to access or misuse data if they manage to breach the system. In addition to encryption, organizations should employ data anonymization techniques whenever possible. Anonymizing data removes personally identifiable information (PII), rendering the data less valuable in case of a breach. For example, if an AI model is being trained using customer data, anonymizing that data ensures that even if the dataset is exposed, it cannot be traced back to any specific individual.

- **Access Controls and Auditing**: Effective access controls are critical for ensuring that only authorized individuals or systems can access sensitive data. This means restricting access based on roles, ensuring that employees and AI systems can only access the data necessary for their tasks. Implementing role-based access controls (RBAC) helps enforce this

165

principle. Additionally, organizations must maintain comprehensive auditing systems that track who accessed the data, when it was accessed, and what actions were taken. This helps detect any unauthorized access or misuse of data. For instance, regular auditing can help identify if an employee improperly accessed sensitive customer data or if a system was compromised by an external attacker.

- **AI-Specific Security Protocols**: AI systems themselves are vulnerable to targeted attacks, such as adversarial attacks, where malicious actors manipulate the input data in ways that can deceive AI models. For example, an attacker might subtly alter the features of an image to fool an AI-powered facial recognition system into misidentifying individuals. To mitigate such threats, organizations should implement AI-specific security protocols, such as adversarial training, which involves exposing the AI model to potential attack scenarios during training to make it more resilient. Other measures, like robustness testing and continuous model monitoring, are also essential to detect and prevent vulnerabilities that could be exploited by attackers.

6.2.3 Data Privacy and Security in AI Governance

Beyond the technical measures outlined above, organizations should also foster a culture of privacy and security within their AI governance framework. This involves appointing data protection officers or privacy officers, developing robust privacy policies, and establishing clear guidelines for handling personal and sensitive data within AI applications.

Furthermore, businesses should conduct regular privacy impact assessments (PIAs) to evaluate the potential risks associated with new AI projects and ensure compliance with privacy laws. Transparency about how AI systems process data and regular communication with stakeholders regarding privacy practices help build confidence and trust in the organization's AI initiatives.

Safeguarding data privacy and security is critical to the ethical deployment of AI systems. By adhering to data privacy regulations, implementing strong security measures, and addressing specific challenges related to AI, organizations can build trust with users and ensure the responsible use of personal data.

As AI technology continues to evolve, the importance of maintaining robust data privacy and security practices will only grow, making it a fundamental aspect of any AI initiative.

6.3 Developing Responsible AI Frameworks

Developing a responsible AI framework is crucial for ensuring that AI systems are deployed in a manner that is ethical, transparent, and aligned with the values and mission of the organization. This framework serves as a guide for every stage of an AI project, from its initial conceptualization and design through to its deployment and ongoing monitoring.

A responsible AI framework ensures that AI technologies are not only technologically sound but also socially responsible, fostering trust among stakeholders and reducing the risk of unintended negative consequences. With the growing integration of AI into diverse sectors, it is essential that organizations have clearly defined structures in place to govern AI usage, ensuring that its impact remains positive and adheres to ethical standards.

6.3.1 Establishing Ethical AI Guidelines

The first step in creating a responsible AI framework is the development of ethical guidelines that outline the organization's standards and values for AI systems.

These guidelines should serve as the ethical backbone for all AI-related initiatives, ensuring that the technology operates in a way that reflects the organization's commitment to societal well-being and fairness. The following key principles should guide the creation of these guidelines:

- **Prioritize Human Rights and Fairness**: AI systems should be designed with a clear focus on upholding fundamental human rights, including privacy, freedom from discrimination, and fairness. This entails addressing biases that could lead to discriminatory outcomes, ensuring that AI does not perpetuate existing societal inequalities. For example, in hiring algorithms, AI systems should be built to avoid bias based on gender, race, or other protected characteristics, ensuring that job candidates are evaluated solely on their qualifications. Organizations should also ensure that AI's decision-making processes do not inadvertently disadvantage vulnerable groups, striving to create solutions that contribute to a more just and equitable society.

- **Promote Transparency and Accountability**: One of the fundamental principles of responsible AI is ensuring transparency. AI systems must operate in a way that is understandable to all stakeholders. This includes ensuring that users, developers, and regulators can comprehend how AI models make decisions, particularly when these decisions impact individuals' lives, such as in healthcare, lending, or criminal justice. Transparency can be achieved through the use of explainable AI (XAI) techniques, where models and their outputs are interpretable. Moreover, accountability mechanisms should be incorporated into the AI lifecycle to hold both human and machine actors responsible for the actions of the system. This means defining clear roles for oversight and establishing processes for addressing errors, biases, or unintended consequences that may arise after deployment.

- **Encourage Inclusivity and Equity**: Responsible AI must be designed to benefit all stakeholders, including marginalized or historically disadvantaged groups. It should actively promote inclusivity, avoiding any forms of exclusion or harm. For example, AI applications in healthcare should consider access to care for underserved communities, ensuring that these groups are not overlooked or disadvantaged. Inclusivity also extends to the design and implementation of AI systems that should be accessible to people with diverse abilities and backgrounds. Equity considerations should also address the societal impact of AI on employment, economic disparities, and access to essential services, ensuring that AI's benefits are widely distributed and not concentrated among already privileged groups.

6.3.2 Creating an AI Ethics Board or Governance Committee

To ensure that AI systems are developed and deployed responsibly, it is essential to establish an internal AI ethics board or governance committee. This body should be made up of a diverse group of stakeholders from various departments and backgrounds, including data scientists, ethicists, legal experts, business leaders, and representatives from affected communities.

The committee's role is to oversee the ethical implications of AI development and use throughout the lifecycle of AI projects. This ensures that AI technologies align with organizational values and comply with ethical guidelines, while also addressing potential risks and impacts on stakeholders. The following tasks should fall within the purview of the ethics board or governance committee:

- **Reviewing AI Projects**: The committee should evaluate the ethical implications of AI initiatives at the inception stage and during development. This process involves assessing the purpose of the AI system, its potential impacts on stakeholders, and the risks it might pose to privacy, fairness, and equity. The committee should also ensure that the design of the AI system follows the ethical principles outlined in the organization's guidelines, particularly focusing on human rights, fairness, and accountability. Regular ethical reviews throughout the development process will help mitigate potential issues early on, preventing the deployment of biased or harmful AI systems.

- **Ensuring Continuous Compliance**: Ethical oversight should not end once an AI system is deployed. The AI ethics board must ensure that AI systems continue to operate in accordance with ethical guidelines throughout their lifecycle. This includes monitoring outcomes and performance, reviewing any unintended consequences, and addressing emerging issues as AI systems interact with real-world data and users. The committee should conduct periodic assessments of AI systems to ensure that they remain in compliance with ethical standards, legal requirements, and organizational values. They should also be responsible for revising guidelines and practices based on new developments in AI technology and emerging societal concerns.

- **Engaging External Experts and Stakeholders**: To ensure that the AI system aligns not only with internal organizational values but also with broader societal norms and legal standards, it is beneficial to engage with external experts, including ethicists, legal advisors, policymakers, regulators, and advocacy groups. These stakeholders can provide valuable perspectives on how AI systems affect the wider community and help to identify potential risks that may not be immediately apparent within the organization. External consultations can also help align AI initiatives with global best practices and ensure that the organization's AI efforts contribute positively to the broader societal conversation around AI ethics. For example, external input might highlight unintended societal impacts, such as algorithmic discrimination or the erosion of privacy, prompting necessary adjustments before issues escalate.

6.3.3 Fostering a Culture of Responsibility in AI

In addition to formalizing these ethical guidelines and governance structures, organizations must foster a culture of responsibility around AI development and deployment. This involves educating employees at all levels about the ethical considerations of AI and ensuring that AI ethics is integrated into the organization's broader culture. Regular training, workshops, and discussions can help raise awareness about the importance of ethical AI and empower employees to raise concerns or suggest improvements.

By embedding these principles into the fabric of the organization, businesses can ensure that AI is developed and deployed in ways that prioritize human well-being, fairness, and accountability. By integrating ethical guidelines, establishing governance committees, and engaging with diverse stakeholders, organizations can build and maintain AI systems that are not only technologically advanced but also socially responsible and aligned with core human values.

6.4 Compliance and Regulatory Considerations

As artificial intelligence technologies continue to advance and permeate various sectors, the potential societal, ethical, and economic impacts are becoming increasingly significant. Governments and regulatory bodies around the world are recognizing these challenges and are enacting laws to address AI's influence.

Organizations implementing AI must remain vigilant in understanding and adhering to these regulations to avoid legal liabilities, reputational damage, and operational disruptions. This necessitates a proactive approach to compliance and regulatory monitoring, ensuring that AI initiatives align with evolving legal frameworks and best practices.

6.4.1 Understanding the Global Regulatory Landscape

The global regulatory environment surrounding AI is diverse, as different regions respond to the technological advancements at varying paces and with different priorities. As AI systems operate across borders, organizations must ensure their compliance with both local and international regulations. Key regulatory frameworks that businesses should monitor include:

- **The EU AI Act**: One of the most comprehensive and forward-thinking regulatory frameworks, the EU AI Act is designed to regulate AI development and deployment within the European Union. It introduces a risk-based classification of AI systems, with stricter oversight for high-risk applications such as biometric data processing, facial recognition, and critical infrastructure automation. For example, AI systems that directly affect public safety or health—such as autonomous vehicles or AI used in healthcare diagnostics—are subject to more stringent requirements, including transparency, human oversight, and risk management. The EU AI Act emphasizes the importance of ensuring that AI technologies are safe, transparent, and in line with EU values, particularly with respect to data privacy and non-discrimination.

- **The California Consumer Privacy Act (CCPA)**: In the United States, state-level data privacy regulations such as the CCPA have a significant impact on how organizations manage personal data. The CCPA grants consumers various rights over their personal data, including the right to know what data is being collected, the right to access that data, and the right to request the deletion of their data. For businesses using AI, this means they must be transparent about the data they collect, ensure they are processing it in accordance with the law, and put in place measures to prevent unauthorized access. Additionally, the CCPA includes provisions around data sale, meaning organizations must give consumers the ability to opt out of their data being sold to third parties, which may include third-party AI service providers.

- **China's AI Governance Framework**: China has developed a set of guidelines focused on the ethical development and regulation of AI, with an emphasis on ensuring that AI technologies align with national priorities, including social stability and security. The Chinese government has issued regulations related to the ethical use of AI in various sectors, such as the tech industry, education, and healthcare, emphasizing the importance of controlling the influence of AI on society. This framework stresses the need for algorithms to be transparent, accountable, and controllable, particularly in applications that affect the public or national security. For instance, AI used for facial recognition and surveillance is heavily scrutinized under these regulations.

Given the complexity of these regulatory environments, organizations must stay informed about both current and emerging AI laws in each region where they operate. Compliance efforts should consider factors such as data protection, safety, bias mitigation, transparency, and ethical considerations to avoid violations and costly fines.

6.4.2 Preparing for Audits and Regulatory Scrutiny

As AI systems are integrated into more critical and sensitive domains, they are becoming subject to increased regulatory scrutiny. Regulators are now looking closely at AI applications in areas such as healthcare, finance, law enforcement, and education, where AI decisions can have far-reaching consequences on individuals and society.

This increased scrutiny means that organizations must be prepared for audits and potential regulatory investigations to ensure they comply with applicable laws. To effectively manage this evolving landscape, organizations should take several preparatory steps:

- **Maintain Transparency and Documentation**: One of the most important practices in preparing for audits is maintaining clear and detailed documentation of the AI system's lifecycle. This includes recording the system's design process, data sources, training methodologies, and the logic behind the decision-making processes. Keeping detailed logs about the system's governance mechanisms, such as ethical review procedures, algorithmic audits, and bias mitigation strategies, can provide valuable insights during regulatory reviews. This transparency not only facilitates regulatory audits but also enables organizations to demonstrate that their AI systems are being developed and deployed in compliance with legal and ethical standards.

- **Develop Compliance Plans**: Organizations should create comprehensive compliance plans that explicitly outline how they will ensure that their AI systems comply with all relevant laws and regulations. These plans should include regular compliance audits, risk assessments, and periodic reviews of AI systems to ensure ongoing adherence to privacy and security standards. Moreover, the plan should also address how the organization will respond in the event of a regulatory inquiry or violation. This could involve establishing a crisis management protocol to mitigate the impact of non-compliance, as well as a process for notifying regulators and affected individuals if a breach occurs.

- **Establish Employee Training Programs**: AI compliance requires the active participation of various stakeholders across the organization, from data scientists and AI engineers to legal teams and business managers. Training programs that educate employees about the legal, ethical, and operational aspects of AI compliance are critical. These programs should focus on key topics, including understanding the regulations governing AI, identifying potential compliance risks, and the steps to take in ensuring that AI systems are developed and deployed in a compliant manner. Additionally, regular workshops or training sessions can be used to keep employees up to date on the latest changes in AI regulation, ensuring the organization is always prepared to respond to evolving regulatory standards.

- **Prepare for Ongoing Regulatory Engagement**: Regulatory bodies are continually refining AI-related laws, and new regulations are likely to emerge as AI technologies evolve. Organizations should stay proactive by engaging with policymakers, participating in industry forums, and contributing to discussions about the future of AI regulation. By doing so, businesses can not only ensure they are meeting current compliance standards but also anticipate future regulatory trends, enabling them to stay ahead of the curve. Regular engagement with regulatory bodies can also help build a positive reputation for the organization as a responsible and ethical AI practitioner.

Organizations must prioritize compliance with a growing body of regulations to mitigate legal risks and maintain public trust.

By staying informed about the regulatory landscape, preparing for audits, and implementing robust compliance plans, businesses can ensure their AI systems are operating in a lawful, ethical, and transparent manner. This proactive approach to compliance will not only help avoid legal pitfalls but also enhance the organization's credibility as a responsible AI innovator.

Ethical governance and risk management are critical pillars of successful AI adoption. To ensure that AI systems are used responsibly, organizations must actively address bias, maintain transparency, and prioritize privacy and security. Developing a responsible AI framework, adhering to regulatory standards, and implementing strong governance practices will not only mitigate risks but also enhance trust and accountability within the organization and with external stakeholders.

Chapter 7: Organizational Change Management

The adoption of generative AI technologies is not merely a technical challenge; it is a profound organizational shift that requires careful planning, leadership commitment, and a strategy for overcoming resistance to change. Implementing AI at scale can impact everything from corporate culture and workforce dynamics to operational processes and customer relations.

Without a clear and thoughtful approach to organizational change management (OCM), even the most promising AI initiatives can falter, stymied by employee resistance, lack of clarity, or insufficient buy-in.

This chapter explores the key components of a successful organizational change strategy, highlighting how to engage leadership, prepare the workforce, communicate effectively, and foster a culture that embraces the transformative power of AI. From securing executive commitment to building AI literacy across the organization, OCM is essential for aligning AI investments with business goals and ensuring the long-term success of AI initiatives.

7.1 Securing Leadership Commitment

Organizational change, particularly in the context of adopting advanced technologies like AI, begins with the commitment and active participation of leadership. The success of AI initiatives hinges on whether senior executives are fully invested in driving the change, aligning it with the organization's broader strategic objectives, and providing the necessary resources and support. Without this commitment from the top, AI projects are at risk of being sidelined, underfunded, or not properly integrated into the overall business strategy.

7.1.1 Defining a Clear Vision for AI

For AI initiatives to thrive, leadership must articulate a clear and compelling vision that resonates with the organization's overarching goals. This vision should not only highlight the technical aspects of AI but also demonstrate how AI aligns with and drives broader business objectives.

A clear vision helps frame AI as a strategic enabler—one that enhances operational efficiency, fosters innovation, improves customer experiences, and creates new revenue opportunities.

A well-articulated vision can generate excitement and buy-in from employees at all levels of the organization. When leadership can clearly connect AI adoption with key business goals, it empowers teams across departments to see how AI can drive tangible improvements and achieve shared success. It also helps mitigate concerns around AI's perceived complexity or potential disruption by positioning it as a tool that will enhance, rather than replace, existing operations.

For example, a manufacturing company might frame AI adoption as a means of revolutionizing production forecasting, optimizing supply chains, and reducing downtime—aligning with the broader goals of operational excellence, cost reduction, and continuous improvement. By framing AI in these terms, leadership ensures that AI is viewed not as a technological experiment, but as an essential strategy for achieving business success.

7.1.2 Establishing a Governance Structure

Once the vision for AI is clearly defined, the next crucial step is to establish a governance structure that ensures strategic alignment and accountability throughout the execution of AI initiatives. AI governance is vital for maintaining oversight, ensuring compliance with ethical standards, and ensuring that AI projects are executed efficiently and effectively.

A robust governance framework provides a clear pathway for decision-making, resource allocation, and addressing challenges as they arise.

A typical AI governance structure includes several key components:

- **AI Steering Committees**: These cross-functional teams of senior leaders are responsible for overseeing the overall progress of AI initiatives within the organization. Steering committees ensure that AI projects remain aligned with strategic goals, allocate necessary resources, and resolve any roadblocks that may emerge. This committee also plays an integral role in assessing the risks and returns of AI investments and making adjustments to the course of action as needed.

- **Executive Champions**: Appointing specific C-suite executives to champion individual AI projects signals to the organization that AI adoption is a top priority. These champions take ownership of AI initiatives, providing leadership, oversight, and strategic direction. Having an executive champion for each project ensures that there is a clear point of accountability, which is essential for making critical decisions, securing necessary resources, and keeping the project on track. Executive champions also play a crucial role in rallying support and removing obstacles to success, helping to maintain momentum and demonstrate leadership commitment.

7.1.3 Allocating Resources for AI Initiatives

Securing sufficient resources is one of the most critical elements for successful AI implementation. AI projects require not only substantial financial investment but also human resources with the right expertise. Ensuring that AI initiatives are adequately funded and supported by the necessary talent is a primary responsibility of senior leadership.

Leaders should allocate resources to a few key areas:

- **Financial Resources**: Investing in AI technology, infrastructure, and research and development is essential. This includes funding for AI tools, platforms, data management systems, and computing power, as well as investing in new AI capabilities and innovations. Budgeting for these resources upfront ensures that the project won't face financial constraints that could undermine its success.

- **Talent Acquisition and Upskilling**: AI initiatives demand specialized skills, so securing the right talent is crucial. Leadership must ensure that the organization has access to skilled data scientists, machine learning engineers, and AI specialists, either through hiring new talent or upskilling current employees. This may involve investing in training programs to equip existing staff with the necessary AI knowledge and ensuring that there is sufficient talent to support the scale of the AI projects. Upskilling initiatives also demonstrate the organization's commitment to the growth and development of its workforce, creating a more adaptive and resilient team.

- **Cross-Departmental Support**: AI projects cannot succeed in isolation, so it is vital that leaders ensure adequate support from all relevant departments. For instance, IT and operations teams need to work closely with AI developers to integrate AI solutions into existing workflows. Marketing, finance, customer service, and other departments must also align their processes with AI-driven strategies to maximize the benefits. Effective resource allocation involves ensuring that these departments are equipped with the tools, training, and collaboration structures needed to work with AI initiatives.

7.1.4 Measuring and Communicating Progress

Once AI projects are underway, senior leadership must not only track the progress of these initiatives but also communicate their success to the wider organization. Transparent and regular communication reinforces the importance of AI within the organization and helps build confidence in its potential.

- **Key Performance Indicators (KPIs)**: Establishing and measuring the right KPIs is essential to understanding the impact of AI projects. KPIs could include operational metrics such as improved efficiency, cost reduction, or revenue growth, as well as more qualitative metrics like employee engagement or customer satisfaction. These indicators help leadership assess whether the AI initiative is meeting expectations and driving the desired outcomes.

- **Celebrating Wins and Adjusting Strategies**: Regularly communicating the successes and milestones of AI initiatives serves to motivate the team, validate the investment, and reinforce the organization's commitment to AI-driven transformation. At the same time, leaders must also be transparent about any challenges or failures, adjusting strategies and reallocating resources when necessary to ensure long-term success. Celebrating wins not only boosts morale but also strengthens the culture of innovation and continuous improvement within the organization.

7.2 Change Communication Strategies

Effective communication plays a critical role in ensuring the success of any organizational transformation, especially when introducing complex, disruptive technologies such as artificial intelligence (AI).

For AI adoption to be successful, employees must grasp not only the technical details but also the underlying reasons for its implementation, how it aligns with the organization's strategic objectives, and the specific ways in which it will affect their daily work and personal responsibilities.

Without a clear understanding of these elements, resistance to change can arise, hindering progress and diminishing the potential benefits of AI.

7.2.1 Building a Transparent Communication Plan

A transparent and consistent communication plan is key to aligning all stakeholders and maintaining trust throughout the AI implementation process. This plan should be structured to facilitate ongoing dialogue and foster a positive attitude toward change. It includes the following essential components:

1. **Clear Messaging**: The messaging about AI adoption should be straightforward, focusing on its strategic significance and the specific business outcomes it will drive. Rather than getting bogged down in technical jargon, the communication should emphasize how AI will generate tangible business value. For example, AI might be framed as a tool that improves operational efficiency, streamlines workflows, enhances customer satisfaction, or drives innovation. Presenting AI in this light ensures that all employees, regardless of their technical expertise, understand its role in the broader organizational context.

2. **Regular Updates**: Keeping employees informed about the progress of AI projects through regular updates is crucial for maintaining engagement and enthusiasm. Updates should be clear and consistent, with a focus on milestones achieved, lessons learned, and any adjustments made to the original plans. Sharing success stories and showcasing tangible results from AI pilot programs can also help build momentum and demonstrate that the technology is delivering real value.

3. **Two-Way Communication**: For effective change management, communication must be a two-way street. It's essential to encourage feedback from employees at all levels, addressing concerns, answering questions, and gathering insights. This can be achieved through open forums, town halls, Q&A sessions, or even digital surveys. When employees feel they have a voice in the process, it helps build trust, reduce resistance, and foster a more collaborative approach to AI adoption.

7.2.2 Tailored Messaging for Different Stakeholders

Different audiences within the organization will have different concerns and needs when it comes to AI adoption. Tailoring messages to specific stakeholder groups is critical for ensuring that the communication resonates with them. Here's how messaging can be tailored for different groups:

1. **Executives and Senior Leaders**: For the C-suite and senior leadership, focus on the strategic impact of AI, how it aligns with the organization's long-term vision, and the return on investment (ROI). Emphasize how AI can provide a competitive edge, enhance market positioning, and help achieve key performance targets. Providing a clear link between AI adoption and the company's strategic objectives will ensure that leaders stay aligned and champion the cause.

2. **Middle Managers**: Middle managers are typically the bridge between senior leadership and front-line employees. For them, it's essential to highlight how AI will support team efficiency, streamline decision-making processes, and drive productivity. Managers should be given the tools and knowledge to communicate these benefits to their teams, so they can help alleviate concerns, set expectations, and encourage adoption. Ensuring that middle managers feel confident in the technology's impact will foster smooth implementation at the operational level.

3. **Front-line Employees**: Front-line employees are often the most directly impacted by AI, especially if there are concerns about job displacement or changes to daily tasks. Therefore, messaging should emphasize how AI is not a replacement for human workers, but a tool to assist them in their roles. AI should be presented as a means of reducing repetitive, mundane tasks, thereby allowing employees to focus on higher-value work. It's also important to highlight the opportunities for skill development and how AI will empower employees to perform their jobs more effectively.

By tailoring communication to the specific needs and concerns of each stakeholder group, organizations can ensure that everyone is on the same page and understands their role in the AI transformation.

7.2.3 Managing Expectations

A critical part of successful AI adoption is managing expectations. AI is a powerful tool, but it is not a magic bullet. Overpromising results or rushing the implementation can lead to disappointment and loss of confidence. It is vital to set realistic goals, define clear milestones, and communicate the timeframes for achieving measurable results.

Managing expectations upfront and maintaining transparency about the challenges and limitations of AI ensures that stakeholders understand the journey ahead and are more likely to remain patient and committed as the technology matures.

Moreover, creating a culture of continuous learning and improvement is essential. Employees should be encouraged to see AI not as a one-time change but as an ongoing process of refinement. Providing regular updates on progress and adapting the technology to better meet organizational needs will help reinforce trust in AI's long-term benefits.

By emphasizing transparency, encouraging two-way communication, tailoring messages for different stakeholders, and managing expectations effectively, organizations can lay the groundwork for a smooth, successful AI implementation.

7.3 Workforce Preparation and Adoption

The successful adoption of AI within an organization hinges on the readiness of the workforce to not only operate new tools but also embrace the significant shifts that AI brings to everyday business processes. Preparing employees for this transition is crucial for overcoming resistance, ensuring smooth integration of AI technologies, and ultimately maximizing their value. Organizations that invest in workforce preparation are more likely to see the positive effects of AI adoption, including improved efficiency, innovation, and employee satisfaction.

7.3.1 Upskilling and Reskilling Programs

To ensure that employees are adequately prepared for an AI-driven future, organizations must implement upskilling and reskilling programs. These programs should be comprehensive, addressing both the technical competencies required to work directly with AI technologies and the broader soft skills necessary to adapt to new ways of working.

1. **Technical Skills:** For employees who will directly interact with AI tools—such as data scientists, machine learning engineers, and AI model developers—providing specialized training in areas like machine learning, data analytics, AI model development, and algorithm optimization is essential. Many companies collaborate with educational institutions, training providers, or online platforms to offer certifications and courses in these technical

areas. Organizations can also create in-house boot camps or workshops to ensure that employees receive hands-on, practical training that matches the company's specific needs. This ensures that the workforce has the knowledge to create, deploy, and maintain AI solutions effectively.

2. **Soft Skills**: Beyond technical expertise, there is a growing recognition that soft skills are just as crucial when integrating AI into an organization. Employees must be equipped to navigate the changes AI will bring to their daily roles. Providing training in areas such as communication, problem-solving, teamwork, and adaptability helps employees work alongside AI systems and leverage their capabilities. For example, AI might handle data analysis, but employees will still need to interpret the results and make strategic decisions based on them. Training on emotional intelligence and change management will also help employees adjust to AI-driven transformations, fostering a mindset that sees AI as an enabler rather than a disruptor.

7.3.2 Developing a Knowledge Sharing Culture

As AI technologies are constantly evolving, keeping the workforce updated on the latest tools, techniques, and industry trends is vital. Creating a culture of continuous learning helps employees stay engaged and proactive in adapting to AI advancements. A culture of knowledge sharing can help employees learn from each other's experiences and discover new ways to use AI effectively within their roles.

1. **Internal Knowledge Sharing**: Encouraging employees to share their insights and lessons learned from AI projects can greatly enhance the collective knowledge within an organization. This can be done through internal seminars, webinars, or workshops, where teams can discuss their AI-related experiences and best practices. Platforms like intranet systems, knowledge management tools, and collaborative forums can also facilitate easy sharing of resources and knowledge. For instance, a data analyst who developed a successful AI model for predicting customer behavior could share their approach and methodologies with other teams working on similar problems, leading to more effective and efficient solutions across the organization.

2. **External Learning Opportunities**: In addition to internal knowledge-sharing initiatives, organizations should support employees in attending external training sessions, AI conferences, webinars, and workshops. These events provide opportunities for employees to learn from thought leaders, stay abreast of the latest research and trends, and network with peers in the AI community. By investing in external learning opportunities, companies foster a growth-oriented mindset and ensure their workforce remains competitive and skilled in a rapidly changing field.

7.3.3 Job Redesign and AI Augmentation

One of the common concerns surrounding AI adoption is the fear of job displacement. However, rather than replacing human workers, AI should be viewed as a tool that enhances existing roles by automating mundane tasks and augmenting human capabilities. By strategically redesigning jobs and focusing on AI augmentation, organizations can create opportunities for employees to engage in higher-value work that requires creativity, decision-making, and emotional intelligence.

1. **Job Redesign Initiatives**: Leaders should work to identify areas where AI can take over repetitive or

time-consuming tasks, such as data entry, routine customer service inquiries, or basic administrative duties. This allows employees to focus on more complex and fulfilling tasks that demand critical thinking, innovation, and strategic decision-making. For example, AI may handle data analysis and generate reports, but employees can spend more time interpreting the insights, collaborating with colleagues, and developing strategies to act on the findings. This shift can improve job satisfaction, boost employee engagement, and lead to a more productive and empowered workforce.

2. **AI Augmentation for Creativity and Decision-Making**: In many industries, AI can be used to complement human creativity and enhance decision-making processes. For instance, in marketing, AI tools can analyze customer behavior and recommend personalized content, while employees can use this information to craft compelling campaigns that resonate with the target audience. By using AI as a supportive tool, employees can focus on higher-order tasks like building relationships, making nuanced decisions, and devising innovative solutions. This approach not only improves productivity but also

fosters a sense of purpose and fulfillment among employees, as they see how AI augments their abilities rather than replacing them.

7.3.4 Fostering Employee Buy-In Through Training and Involvement

A critical component of workforce preparation is fostering employee buy-in. Engaging employees early in the process, involving them in pilot programs, and offering continuous opportunities for training and feedback helps them feel more confident and excited about the changes AI brings.

When employees feel empowered and informed, they are more likely to embrace AI as a helpful tool rather than view it as a threat. By maintaining transparency, creating a supportive learning environment, and involving employees in the evolution of AI projects, organizations can cultivate a positive attitude toward AI adoption across all levels of the workforce.

By focusing on upskilling and reskilling programs, fostering a culture of knowledge sharing, and emphasizing job redesign and AI augmentation, organizations can effectively prepare their workforce for the future. This proactive approach not only ensures that employees are equipped to succeed in an

AI-powered environment but also helps secure the long-term success of AI initiatives within the company.

7.4 Overcoming Resistance and Building AI Literacy

Resistance to change is an inherent part of human nature, and the introduction of AI within an organization often triggers feelings of uncertainty, especially when employees fear job displacement or feel overwhelmed by the complexity of new technologies. Overcoming this resistance requires a strategic approach that addresses concerns directly while also fostering a culture of trust, collaboration, and open communication. This process involves not only managing anxiety but also creating a positive narrative around AI that empowers employees to embrace the changes.

7.4.1 Addressing Fear of Job Displacement

One of the most pervasive concerns surrounding AI adoption is the fear that automation will result in significant job losses. While it's true that AI can automate certain repetitive or low-skill tasks, the technology also has the potential to create new roles, opportunities, and career paths within the organization.

To alleviate fears and shift the perspective on AI, it's essential to communicate the following:

- **AI as an Enabler, Not a Replacement**: Reinforce the message that AI is designed to complement human skills and capabilities. Rather than replacing jobs, AI can be a powerful tool that handles mundane and time-consuming tasks, allowing employees to focus on more creative, strategic, and high-value work. By presenting AI as an assistant rather than a replacement, organizations can ease concerns and highlight the positive impact it can have on daily work.

- **Promoting Career Growth and New Opportunities**: Employees should be reassured that they will not be left behind by the advent of AI. By emphasizing the organization's commitment to upskilling and reskilling, leaders can offer a path forward for employees to grow within the company. These opportunities might include training programs that allow workers to gain new skills in data science, machine learning, or AI management, empowering them to take on new, higher-level responsibilities that AI alone cannot perform.

7.4.2 Building AI Literacy Across the Organization

AI literacy is crucial for ensuring that employees are not just passive participants in the AI adoption process but active contributors who feel confident in using AI tools to enhance their work. To effectively build AI literacy, organizations should take a comprehensive, inclusive approach to education and training:

- **Provide Basic AI Training**: Begin by offering introductory courses on AI that explain its core concepts in clear, simple terms. The goal is to ensure that every employee understands the fundamentals of AI—what it is, how it works, and the specific ways it will impact their roles. These courses should be accessible and free from technical jargon, so all employees, regardless of their technical background, can engage with the material.

- **Create a Culture of Peer Learning and Mentorship**: Building AI literacy doesn't have to be a top-down initiative. Encourage employees with AI expertise or technical experience to mentor their colleagues, fostering a peer-to-peer learning environment. This not only accelerates understanding of AI but also builds trust within teams, as employees feel supported by their peers in navigating the transition. Establishing informal learning groups or AI "champions" within the company can help spread knowledge more effectively.

- **Leverage Interactive Learning Opportunities**: In addition to formal training, consider offering hands-on workshops, simulation exercises, and real-world case studies. These practical learning opportunities allow employees to engage with AI technologies directly, reducing fear and boosting their confidence. By experiencing AI in action, employees are more likely to see its value and understand how it can be integrated into their day-to-day work.

7.4.3 Promoting a Growth Mindset

Encouraging a growth mindset is critical for overcoming resistance to change, particularly in relation to AI adoption. A growth mindset fosters the belief that abilities and skills can be developed through effort, learning, and persistence. Leaders should:

- **Reassure Employees About Continuous Improvement**: Frame AI adoption as a long-term journey of growth and improvement rather than a one-time change. Communicate that AI is not a one-off implementation but an evolving, continuous process that will enhance the organization's capabilities over time. Leaders should emphasize the ongoing learning and adaptability required to stay ahead in the AI landscape, reassuring employees that the company is committed to supporting them throughout the transition.

- **Highlight AI's Role in Personal Development**: Stress the idea that AI adoption is not just a corporate strategy, but also a personal development opportunity for employees. As AI reshapes the organization, employees will be expected to take on new challenges and develop new skills, which can lead to greater job satisfaction, career advancement, and personal growth. By aligning AI adoption with employees' personal and professional growth, organizations can create an environment where employees feel motivated to embrace change and contribute to the company's AI journey.

By addressing resistance, providing robust training, and promoting a culture of growth, organizations can transform AI adoption from a challenge into a shared opportunity for everyone. This holistic approach to workforce preparation ensures that employees are not just capable of using new tools, but are also motivated to engage with AI technologies, driving the company's success in the AI-powered future.

Successful organizational change management is central to AI adoption. Securing leadership commitment, developing clear communication strategies, preparing the workforce, and overcoming resistance are all vital components of a strategy that ensures AI is successfully integrated.

By focusing on these pillars, businesses can reduce friction during the AI transition, increase adoption rates, and foster a culture of innovation that thrives in an AI-powered future. The goal is to create an environment where employees are not just using AI but are actively engaged in shaping how AI evolves within their organization.

Chapter 8: Measuring and Optimizing AI Value

As businesses continue to heavily invest in generative AI technologies, understanding how to assess and quantify the success of these initiatives is becoming increasingly critical.

With AI's growing role in driving business transformation, organizations must ensure that the technologies they implement are delivering tangible and measurable results. Whether AI is being deployed to streamline internal operations, enhance customer experiences, or create innovative new products and services, it is essential for companies to track its impact in a way that justifies the ongoing investment.

This means not only setting clear objectives for AI deployment but also establishing key performance indicators (KPIs) that align with business goals and can be used to assess the return on investment (ROI) of AI initiatives.

This chapter delves into the methods organizations can use to effectively measure the success of their AI efforts. It explores how businesses can continuously optimize AI applications, ensuring that they evolve with technological advancements and shifting market demands.

Moreover, it emphasizes the importance of adaptability in AI strategies, helping businesses refine their approaches over time to maximize value. By regularly assessing AI's performance, identifying areas for improvement, and adjusting strategies as necessary, companies can ensure that their AI investments continue to drive significant value and stay aligned with their broader strategic objectives.

8.1 Key Performance Indicators (KPIs)

Key Performance Indicators (KPIs) are an essential tool for businesses to gauge the effectiveness of their AI initiatives. To assess AI's success, organizations must define and track KPIs that align with the specific goals of each AI project. Since AI projects can vary greatly in their objectives and scope—ranging from automation and process optimization to predictive analytics and customer personalization—it is crucial that the KPIs chosen are tailored to reflect the unique goals and expected outcomes of each initiative. For example, an AI initiative focused on automating supply chain processes will have different KPIs compared to one focused on personalizing customer experiences. By selecting the right

KPIs, businesses ensure that they can accurately measure progress and the overall impact of AI projects.

When defining KPIs, it's important to not only measure technical aspects like accuracy, speed, or error rates but also to focus on how AI contributes to the organization's broader business goals. This ensures that AI is delivering measurable value to the company.

For instance, for AI-driven product recommendations or marketing campaigns, KPIs should track metrics like revenue generated or improvements in customer lifetime value (CLV), as these reflect the direct financial impact of AI.

Similarly, for AI applications focused on operational optimization—such as predictive maintenance or process automation—KPIs should include cost savings, operational efficiencies, and time reductions. These types of KPIs are essential to show how AI is contributing to the bottom line by improving processes and reducing waste.

AI solutions that enhance customer service, such as chatbots or recommendation systems, should be assessed based on customer satisfaction metrics, Net Promoter Scores (NPS), response times, and service quality improvements. Additionally, for AI that assists employees in their daily tasks, such as automating repetitive work, employee productivity and reduced task completion times are key performance indicators that reflect the value AI adds in terms of efficiency and employee satisfaction.

To ensure the KPIs are effective in tracking AI success, they must be SMART—Specific, Measurable, Achievable, Relevant, and Time-bound. A SMART KPI provides a clear target, enabling businesses to monitor progress and make adjustments when necessary. For example, rather than just tracking the overall accuracy of an AI model, a SMART KPI might set a clear goal, such as "Increase the customer service chatbot resolution rate by 15% within the next six months." This type of KPI is focused, measurable, and has a clear timeline for achieving the goal.

Different AI use cases also require different types of KPIs to reflect their specific objectives. For operational AI applications, KPIs might focus on improvements in productivity, time savings, error reduction, and cost savings. For predictive analytics, KPIs may center on the accuracy of predictions, reductions in forecasting errors, and shortened lead times. For AI applications that focus on customer experience, important KPIs could include customer engagement rates, customer retention, and conversion rates for personalized recommendations.

Once the appropriate KPIs have been defined, it is essential for organizations to implement systems to track and report on AI performance. This can include real-time dashboards, automated reports, and regular performance reviews to assess how AI initiatives are progressing. These tools enable stakeholders to track the impact of AI projects quickly and effectively, ensuring transparency and accountability.

Regular reporting on KPIs also helps organizations decide whether their AI initiatives are on track, identify any challenges or areas for improvement, and make data-driven decisions on whether to continue with or adjust the AI strategies in place. Through consistent tracking and reporting, businesses can optimize their AI initiatives and ensure that they continue to align with overall business objectives, thereby maximizing the value of their AI investments over time.

8.2 Feedback Loops and Continuous Improvement

Feedback Loops and Continuous Improvement are integral aspects of the AI development lifecycle. One of the standout features of AI is its capacity to evolve and enhance its performance over time by learning from new inputs, experiences, and ongoing feedback. Establishing robust feedback loops is vital to ensuring that AI systems not only meet initial expectations but also improve continuously, adapting to new challenges, data, and user needs. By implementing a structured feedback loop, organizations can foster an environment of ongoing optimization, allowing AI models to stay relevant, accurate, and effective as they operate.

Building a Feedback Loop Framework involves creating a systematic approach that allows the AI system to adjust and improve based on new data or insights. The process begins with **data collection**, where continuous monitoring is critical. Gathering feedback from a range of sources—whether it's user interactions, sensor data from production systems, or customer satisfaction surveys—ensures that the system's performance is evaluated from multiple angles.

Once the data is collected, the next phase is **analysis and evaluation**. Regularly assessing the AI's output ensures that it aligns with business goals. For example, if an AI recommendation engine designed to increase sales is underperforming, this phase would help identify the root causes, such as inadequate data inputs or flawed algorithmic assumptions.

The **model update** phase follows, where AI models are retrained or adjusted based on the findings from the evaluation. This could involve incorporating new training data, tweaking model parameters, or adjusting the algorithm's approach. After updates are made, the AI model must go through **deployment and monitoring**. The updated model should be redeployed to the live environment, with ongoing monitoring to ensure the changes bring about the desired improvements in performance and business outcomes.

Incorporating a **Human-in-the-Loop (HITL)** approach can significantly enhance the quality of feedback and continuous improvement. While AI systems are highly effective at processing large datasets and recognizing patterns, there are areas where human judgment is indispensable, particularly in nuanced decision-making or complex problem-solving. In a HITL setup, human oversight helps refine the model's performance by reviewing AI outputs, offering feedback, and making adjustments when necessary.

This approach is particularly useful for tasks where empathy, emotional intelligence, or contextual understanding is required. For instance, in a customer service AI, feedback from human agents can be used to fine-tune the AI's responses, making them more empathetic, contextually aware, and capable of addressing customer concerns more effectively. Such collaboration ensures that the AI model is consistently aligned with human expectations and organizational standards.

Incorporating **new data and trends** into the feedback loop is also a crucial factor in ensuring that AI systems remain effective and relevant. AI models that are trained on outdated or static data will quickly lose their predictive accuracy and relevance, especially in dynamic industries such as e-commerce, healthcare, or finance.

For example, customer preferences and purchasing behaviors in e-commerce can shift rapidly, necessitating frequent model updates based on real-time data. AI systems must be designed to incorporate fresh, relevant information to continuously enhance their performance and adaptability to changing conditions. As a result, businesses should ensure that the feedback loop not only captures data on current system performance but also anticipates future trends and shifts in the operating environment.

The process of **iterative refinement and scaling** is where continuous improvement truly takes shape. AI models are rarely perfect from the start, and they generally improve incrementally over time. With each round of feedback and model optimization, the system gets closer to its ideal performance. This iterative process is essential for long-term AI success, as it allows organizations to make continuous, data-driven improvements that incrementally refine the AI's capabilities.

Furthermore, organizations should instill a culture of ongoing iteration, where feedback and model adjustments are seen as a regular part of the AI lifecycle rather than a one-time event. As AI systems evolve, this iterative approach ensures that they can scale with increasing complexity, data volume, and business needs, positioning the organization to maximize the long-term value of AI investments.

8.3 Quantifying AI's Business Impact

Beyond evaluating the internal performance of AI systems, organizations must assess the broader business impact that AI initiatives bring. While internal metrics like model accuracy or processing speed are important, the true value of AI is realized when it translates into tangible outcomes that advance the business's goals. This means AI initiatives must contribute to key business drivers such as increasing revenue, reducing operational costs, enhancing customer satisfaction, or fostering innovation.

The challenge lies in effectively measuring and attributing the specific outcomes of AI-driven changes to business success.

Organizations need to adopt strategies for quantifying how AI's performance aligns with financial and operational goals. Only by linking AI outcomes to these core metrics can businesses demonstrate the value of their AI investments and justify further resource allocation.

8.3.1 Calculating ROI (Return on Investment)

One of the most important tasks in assessing AI's business impact is calculating the Return on Investment (ROI). While ROI is a common metric for evaluating the success of investments, calculating it for AI projects presents unique challenges.

AI projects often have long-term benefits that evolve over time, meaning the return may not be immediately apparent. In addition, the initial costs of AI adoption—such as development, infrastructure, and training—can be substantial. Despite these complexities, businesses can estimate ROI by considering both direct and indirect benefits that result from AI investments:

- **Direct Benefits**: These include the clear and measurable financial returns AI projects bring. For example, AI-driven marketing campaigns can directly increase revenue by providing personalized recommendations that lead to more conversions. Additionally, AI-enhanced customer retention strategies can lead to higher lifetime customer value (CLV), thereby boosting long-term revenue streams.

- **Cost Savings**: Many AI applications are designed to reduce costs through automation or optimization. For instance, AI-powered chatbots can automate customer service, reducing the need for human agents and lowering operational expenses. Similarly, AI in supply chain management can streamline processes, reducing waste and lowering inventory costs.

- **Efficiency Gains**: AI can significantly improve operational efficiency by automating repetitive tasks, which saves valuable time. This allows employees to focus on more strategic tasks, thereby improving workforce productivity and increasing the overall output without additional labor costs.

- **Indirect Benefits**: In addition to direct financial benefits, AI can bring intangible or long-term value. For example, AI-powered tools can enhance a company's brand reputation by improving customer experiences. Over time, these improvements can lead to stronger customer loyalty, market differentiation, and higher competitive advantage.

By calculating the costs associated with implementing AI—such as development costs, infrastructure investment, and training expenses—and comparing them to the measurable benefits, businesses can compute ROI. This calculation can help illustrate whether AI is delivering value and justify continued investments.

8.3.2 Business Impact of AI on Key Drivers

To effectively measure the business impact of AI, it's essential to understand how AI initiatives affect key business drivers. These drivers are the core elements that contribute to the company's financial success, market positioning, and operational efficiency. For example:

- **Customer Lifetime Value (CLV)**: AI has a significant impact on customer engagement and retention, which directly influences CLV. AI systems that personalize marketing or recommend products based on customer preferences can increase engagement and repeat purchases, thus enhancing customer loyalty and CLV. A business that uses AI to provide tailored experiences may see a long-term increase in customer retention and revenue growth.

- **Market Share**: AI can also drive innovation by enabling businesses to introduce new products, services, or features that differentiate them from competitors. AI-driven product development or customer insights can lead to more relevant offerings in the market, which can increase a company's market share. For instance, AI-based customer segmentation may reveal previously untapped market segments, allowing a company to capture a larger portion of the market.

- **Operational Efficiency**: One of the most significant ways AI affects business outcomes is through its ability to streamline operations. AI-powered automation can reduce waste, enhance throughput, and eliminate bottlenecks in processes, all of which contribute to improved profitability. AI can also reduce human error, leading to more consistent and reliable operations, further driving efficiency and reducing operational costs.

8.3.3 Attribution Modeling

While AI's impact is often positive, it can be difficult to attribute specific outcomes solely to AI initiatives. AI programs frequently work in conjunction with other business strategies and technologies, making it essential to adopt **attribution modeling** to assess AI's specific contribution. Attribution modeling helps organizations understand the combined effect of multiple factors in achieving business outcomes.

For example, if AI-driven customer segmentation is used alongside a new marketing campaign, attribution modeling can help determine how much of the sales increase is due to AI and how much is attributed to the marketing strategies. By understanding the direct impact of AI in relation to other business efforts, companies can better allocate resources and refine their strategies to maximize AI's contribution.

8.3.4 Long-Term Value Creation

While AI's short-term financial returns are often tracked through metrics like ROI or revenue growth, its long-term value creation can be equally important. AI can provide strategic insights that help companies make better decisions, forecast trends, and improve their competitive positioning over time. The value of AI lies not only in immediate gains but also in its ability to inform long-term strategy.

For example, by analyzing vast amounts of customer data, AI can uncover emerging market trends or new consumer preferences that guide product innovation or market expansion strategies. While the financial impact of these insights might not be realized immediately, they play a crucial role in positioning the company for future success and sustainable growth. As organizations continue to invest in AI, its capacity to drive innovation, improve decision-making, and strengthen market position will become an increasingly important factor in measuring AI's long-term business impact.

8.4 Adaptive Strategy Development

In the fast-paced world of artificial intelligence (AI), success is rarely achieved by sticking to a rigid, one-size-fits-all strategy. AI technologies are continually evolving, and business environments can shift unexpectedly, requiring organizations to remain adaptable. The ability to pivot and adjust strategies over time is critical to realizing the full potential of AI investments.

As AI matures and as organizations gather more experience with these technologies, they must refine their approaches to ensure that AI initiatives continue to align with business goals, drive value, and remain competitive in a rapidly changing marketplace. Adaptive strategy development in AI is not just about flexibility in execution; it also involves reshaping the strategic vision based on insights and data accumulated throughout the journey.

8.4.1 Embracing a Test-and-Learn Approach

A fundamental aspect of adaptive AI strategy is adopting a **test-and-learn** mindset. AI strategies should be viewed as dynamic, allowing for frequent experimentation, feedback collection, and iterative improvements. This approach enables organizations to test AI applications on a smaller scale before committing significant resources to large-scale implementations.

By experimenting with different use cases and evaluating outcomes through controlled trials, businesses can mitigate risks and identify the most promising applications of AI. A test-and-learn approach also facilitates learning from failures, ensuring that organizations do not repeat mistakes and instead grow more informed with each iteration.

For instance, a company could implement an AI-powered customer service chatbot in a specific region or department as a pilot project. During the trial phase, the company would measure key performance indicators (KPIs), such as response time, customer satisfaction, and resolution rates.

Based on this data, the company can adjust the AI model, improve user interfaces, or refine its integration with existing systems. After fine-tuning the solution and ensuring positive results, the company could then expand the AI solution to other regions or departments, scaling it for greater impact. This approach prevents the company from overcommitting before validating the AI's effectiveness and ensures resources are allocated only to high-impact initiatives.

8.4.2 Strategic Flexibility in AI Use Cases

The fast-paced development of AI also means that businesses need to constantly reevaluate their AI use cases. What works today may not be as effective in the future, and initial AI applications might need reworking or refinement. When an AI implementation does not deliver the anticipated results, businesses must be prepared to change course. This is where strategic flexibility becomes crucial. Organizations should be agile enough to pivot toward new AI use cases if existing ones fail to meet business expectations.

For example, a logistics company initially implementing AI to streamline route optimization might discover through trial and feedback that predictive maintenance models offer more immediate and impactful results.

The AI may identify inefficiencies in the maintenance schedule of its fleet, reducing unexpected breakdowns and costly repairs. In this scenario, the company would shift its focus from logistics optimization to predictive maintenance, channeling resources into refining this new use case. This adaptability ensures that AI investments remain aligned with organizational needs, allowing businesses to take advantage of emerging opportunities and avoid stagnation.

8.4.3 Continuous Reassessment of Business Needs

As AI technologies continue to evolve, business priorities may also change, influenced by new market conditions, competitive pressures, or shifts in consumer behavior. To maintain the effectiveness of AI initiatives, companies must regularly reassess their strategic goals and adjust AI deployments to align with these evolving objectives. An AI solution that was initially focused on improving operational efficiency may need to shift towards innovation and product development as the company matures in its AI capabilities.

For instance, a manufacturing company may initially leverage AI to automate repetitive tasks, resulting in significant cost savings and process efficiencies. Once these foundational capabilities are established, the business may realize that the next phase of growth lies in using AI to drive product innovation or enter new markets.

The AI systems that were initially used for cost-saving automation could now be repurposed to support R&D, improve product design, or enhance customer experiences. By continuously reassessing business needs, companies ensure that AI remains a strategic asset, driving the long-term success and growth of the organization.

8.4.4 Agility in Decision-Making

AI initiatives require decision-making that is both agile and data-driven. In the face of rapid technological advancements and unpredictable business environments, companies cannot afford to make decisions based solely on outdated information or rigid plans. Instead, decision-making should be flexible, allowing for quick adjustments when new insights emerge or when performance evaluations highlight areas for improvement. Organizations must build frameworks that facilitate fast, evidence-based decision-making, enabling leaders to act on real-time data.

For example, after investing in an AI-powered marketing solution that isn't producing the desired customer engagement, an organization must be ready to pivot. Instead of adhering to the original plan of expanding the AI solution, the company may choose to adjust the parameters of the AI model, retrain it with new data, or explore alternative AI use cases that are more aligned with customer expectations.

By making decisions in real time, based on measurable performance and user feedback, businesses can maintain momentum and optimize their AI initiatives without waiting for long periods before making adjustments. This adaptability also helps businesses stay ahead of competitors by quickly seizing new opportunities and addressing challenges as they arise.

Chapter 9: Future-Proofing Your AI Strategy

The field of artificial intelligence is evolving at an unprecedented rate, with new breakthroughs, tools, and technologies emerging regularly. To stay competitive and continue benefiting from AI, organizations need to future-proof their AI strategies. This chapter outlines how companies can proactively prepare for the future, ensuring they remain agile, innovative, and ready to capitalize on the next wave of AI advancements.

9.1 Emerging AI Trends

To build a future-proof AI strategy, organizations must stay ahead of the curve by understanding and integrating the latest trends in AI. While AI is already transforming industries, emerging technologies and approaches are set to further revolutionize the landscape. These trends are not just about the evolution of technology but also about understanding how these innovations will reshape industries, customer expectations, and operational models.

1. **Generative AI and Creativity:** Generative AI, which involves the creation of new content (text, images, music, etc.), is becoming a dominant force in many industries. While tools like GPT and DALL·E have already made waves in the creative sectors, we can expect these technologies to become even more sophisticated, capable of handling highly specialized creative tasks across industries like fashion, entertainment, and advertising. Organizations should explore how generative AI can augment human creativity, automate content creation, and even drive innovation in product design.

2. **AI-Driven Personalization at Scale:** Personalization is one of the most impactful use cases of AI, and the next frontier is to apply this technology at an even larger scale. Emerging AI systems are moving beyond simple recommendations to create deeply personalized experiences for users in real-time. For instance, AI could offer tailored learning experiences for employees, generate personalized product designs for customers, or provide real-time, hyper-targeted marketing content. Businesses that can harness AI's ability to personalize customer interactions will have a distinct competitive edge.

3. **Explainable AI (XAI):** As AI becomes more integrated into decision-making processes, the need for explainable AI grows. In many applications, especially those involving critical decisions (e.g., in healthcare or finance), stakeholders need to understand how and why a model made a specific decision. The development of AI models that are transparent and interpretable will help build trust and ensure compliance with regulations. Ensuring explainability in AI models will be essential for businesses to foster transparency, ethical standards, and stakeholder confidence.

4. **AI and Autonomous Systems:** Autonomous systems, powered by AI, are poised to change industries like transportation, logistics, manufacturing, and agriculture. Autonomous vehicles, drones, and robotic systems will continue to evolve, providing new opportunities for cost-saving, efficiency, and safety improvements. Businesses should explore how autonomous AI systems could be integrated into their operations or even create new business models based on autonomous technologies.

5. **AI-Integrated Internet of Things (AIoT):** The integration of AI with IoT (AIoT) devices is another transformative trend. By embedding AI into physical devices, businesses can create smarter, more responsive systems. This is already happening in smart homes, supply chain management, healthcare devices, and manufacturing automation. As more data is collected through IoT devices, AI can help businesses process this information in real-time and make smarter decisions. Preparing for AIoT means understanding how connected devices can optimize operations and enhance customer experiences.

6. **AI and Quantum Computing:** While still in the early stages, quantum computing is set to revolutionize AI by providing immense processing power that could make current AI models obsolete. Quantum computers could process vast amounts of data far more quickly than traditional computers, enabling breakthroughs in machine learning algorithms, optimization problems, and complex simulations. Businesses should keep a close eye on quantum computing developments and be ready to adapt once quantum-enabled AI becomes commercially viable.

9.2 Investment in R&D

To future-proof your AI strategy, consistent investment in Research and Development (R&D) is crucial. Staying at the forefront of AI technology requires not only adopting current innovations but also actively contributing to the future of AI through internal R&D and collaboration with external innovators.

1. **Internal AI Research:** Creating a dedicated AI research division within the organization is one of the most effective ways to ensure that your business remains ahead of emerging trends. These teams can focus on exploring new AI methodologies, experimenting with novel applications, and building prototypes for future AI solutions. Additionally, fostering a research culture helps attract top AI talent and signals to the market that the company is committed to AI innovation.

2. **Partnerships with Academia and Research Institutions:** Collaboration with academic institutions, universities, and AI-focused research centers can provide valuable access to cutting-edge research and emerging technologies. Partnering with academia can offer insights into the latest AI theories

and breakthroughs, as well as access to top-tier talent. Many successful AI startups have emerged from university research labs, making these partnerships crucial for long-term AI strategy development.

3. **External Startups and Innovation Hubs:** In addition to academic partnerships, businesses can explore relationships with AI startups and innovation hubs. These entities often bring disruptive technologies and fresh perspectives that can significantly enhance a company's AI capabilities. Businesses that invest in or collaborate with AI-focused startups can rapidly gain access to new tools, algorithms, and platforms that may otherwise take years to develop internally.

4. **Exploring AI Ethics and Sustainability in R&D:** As AI continues to grow, the ethical considerations around its deployment are becoming more prominent. Researching responsible AI, focusing on fairness, transparency, and environmental sustainability, should be integrated into your R&D investments. Developing AI solutions that are ethically sound and sustainable will not only benefit society but also protect your business from potential backlash or legal issues.

9.3 Building Organizational Agility

AI's rapid pace of innovation means that organizations must be able to adapt quickly to changes in technology, market demands, and regulatory environments. Building organizational agility is one of the most important strategies for future-proofing your AI initiatives.

1. **Flexible AI Governance Models:** An agile AI governance model allows businesses to respond swiftly to technological advancements or changes in the market landscape. This includes flexible processes for evaluating and scaling new AI technologies, adjusting strategies in response to shifting business priorities, and ensuring compliance with evolving regulations. An adaptable governance structure will also enable the organization to pivot or evolve its AI strategy when needed without significant disruption.

2. **Cross-Functional Teams for AI Initiatives:** To stay nimble, businesses should form cross-functional teams that bring together diverse perspectives and expertise. These teams should include AI researchers, business leaders, product managers, engineers, and legal and ethical experts. Cross-

functional collaboration ensures that AI solutions are developed and implemented in alignment with both technological advancements and broader business goals.

3. **Agility in AI Scaling:** The ability to scale AI systems rapidly across the organization is a core aspect of agility. Businesses should prioritize AI platforms and architectures that support scalability. Cloud-based AI platforms, for example, offer organizations the flexibility to scale their AI applications up or down as needed. Furthermore, adopting a modular approach to AI systems allows organizations to implement new tools and capabilities without overhauling existing infrastructure.

4. **Fostering a Culture of Innovation:** Agility isn't just about operational flexibility; it also involves cultivating a mindset of continuous innovation. Encourage employees to experiment, challenge the status quo, and explore new AI applications. This innovation-driven culture will not only help the business stay ahead of technological trends but also ensure that employees are equipped to embrace changes in the business environment.

9.4 Preparing for Rapid Technological Evolution

AI's rapid development means that businesses need to prepare for the future by fostering an environment of constant learning and adaptation. Organizations must be ready to embrace both incremental and disruptive changes in the AI field, and this requires a proactive, forward-thinking approach.

1. **Continuous Skill Development and Training**
   As AI technology evolves, so must the skills of the workforce. Organizations should continuously invest in employee training programs that keep the workforce updated on the latest AI developments. Upskilling and reskilling employees in AI-related fields will ensure that your talent pool remains competitive and capable of handling future AI challenges.

2. **Building Long-Term AI Strategies**
   Future-proofing involves not just reacting to current AI developments but also anticipating where the technology is heading. Develop long-term AI strategies that consider potential advancements in AI and plan for how the organization will leverage them.

For example, if quantum computing is expected to disrupt AI, businesses should explore potential use cases for this technology and begin laying the groundwork to integrate it.

3. **Staying Connected to Industry Networks**
The AI landscape is rapidly evolving, and staying connected with industry networks, thought leaders, and AI-focused conferences will provide insight into emerging trends and developments. Networking with other businesses, AI researchers, and policymakers can help your organization stay informed and prepared for what's to come.

Future-proofing your AI strategy involves understanding emerging trends, investing in ongoing R&D, fostering organizational agility, and preparing for the rapid pace of technological evolution. This proactive approach will help organizations not only survive in a rapidly changing landscape but thrive, continuously innovating and leading in the AI-powered future.

Appendices

The appendices provide additional resources to further enhance your understanding of AI, along with practical tools and frameworks to guide your AI journey. This section serves as a valuable reference for executives and decision-makers who want to deepen their knowledge of AI concepts, stay updated with relevant resources, and utilize frameworks for effective AI strategy implementation.

Glossary of AI Terms

This glossary provides definitions of key AI terms, ensuring that readers can easily navigate the technical terminology often used in discussions about generative AI. Understanding these terms is crucial for both technical and non-technical stakeholders as they engage in AI projects.

- **Artificial Intelligence (AI):** The simulation of human intelligence in machines, enabling them to perform tasks such as learning, reasoning, problem-solving, perception, and language understanding.

- **Machine Learning (ML):** A subset of AI that enables machines to learn from data and improve over time without explicit programming. ML algorithms identify patterns in data and make predictions or decisions based on it.

- **Deep Learning (DL):** A type of machine learning that uses neural networks with many layers (hence "deep") to model complex patterns in large datasets. It is especially effective in tasks such as image recognition, speech processing, and natural language understanding.

- **Generative AI:** AI technologies that create new content, such as text, images, music, or even video, by learning from existing datasets. Examples include GPT for text generation and DALL·E for image creation.

- **Neural Networks:** A network of algorithms that attempts to recognize underlying relationships in a set of data through a process that mimics the way the human brain operates. It forms the backbone of deep learning models.

- **Natural Language Processing (NLP):** A branch of AI that focuses on the interaction between computers and human language. NLP involves tasks such as language translation, sentiment analysis, and text summarization.

- **Reinforcement Learning (RL):** A type of machine learning where an agent learns by interacting with its environment and receiving feedback in the form of rewards or penalties. It is often used in robotics, gaming, and autonomous systems.

- **Ethical AI:** AI systems developed and deployed in a way that aligns with moral principles, ensuring fairness, transparency, and accountability while minimizing biases and harmful impacts.

- **Explainable AI (XAI):** A set of techniques in AI design that enables users to understand and interpret the decisions made by AI models, providing transparency and trustworthiness in AI systems.

- **Transfer Learning:** A technique where a pre-trained model on one task is adapted to a new but related task. This approach allows for more efficient training, especially when data for the new task is limited.

- **Computer Vision:** A field of AI that enables machines to interpret and understand visual information from the world, including images and video. It is used in applications such as facial recognition, object detection, and autonomous driving.

- **Autonomous Systems:** AI systems that can perform tasks or make decisions independently without human intervention, often used in robotics, vehicles, and drones.

- **Data Privacy and Security:** Refers to the protection of personal and sensitive data from unauthorized access, ensuring that AI systems comply with regulations such as GDPR and maintain user trust.

- **AI Ethics:** The study of how AI technologies impact society, with a focus on ensuring that AI is developed and used in a way that is ethical, fair, and aligned with societal values.

- **Edge AI:** The deployment of AI algorithms on local devices (rather than in the cloud) to enable real-time data processing and decision-making. It is used in applications like IoT devices and autonomous vehicles.

- **Synthetic Data:** Data that is artificially generated rather than collected from real-world sources. It is often used in training AI models when real-world data is scarce or too sensitive to use.

- **AI Governance:** The framework of policies, regulations, and oversight mechanisms to guide the ethical development and deployment of AI technologies within an organization.

Assessment Tools and Frameworks

The following tools and frameworks will assist executives in assessing their organization's AI readiness, evaluating potential AI initiatives, and creating a strategic plan for AI integration.

AI Maturity Model

The **AI Maturity Model** is a framework used to assess an organization's progress in adopting and integrating Artificial Intelligence (AI) technologies. It helps businesses understand where they stand in terms of their AI capabilities, how to evaluate their current state, and identify the next steps for growth. The model provides a roadmap for organizations to optimize their AI strategies, ensure they are leveraging AI's full potential, and align AI initiatives with broader business goals. The model typically includes several stages, each representing a different level of AI sophistication, from basic awareness to full AI integration.

Below is an expanded explanation of the typical stages in the **AI Maturity Model:**

1. Initial/Ad Hoc (AI Awareness)

In the **Initial/Ad Hoc** stage, AI is either non-existent within the organization or in its infancy. At this stage, AI adoption is often driven by isolated efforts or pilot projects with no clear strategy or understanding of its business impact. AI might be explored by a single department or small group of employees, and AI technologies might not be fully understood or integrated into everyday operations. The focus is primarily on experimenting with AI tools without a broader, coherent AI strategy.

Characteristics:

- **Limited AI Understanding**: AI is perceived as a tool for experimentation and novelty, with little understanding of its full potential across the organization.

- **Lack of Strategy**: No formal strategy or roadmap for AI integration or long-term vision.

- **Limited Resources**: Few resources dedicated to AI research and implementation, often relying on external consultants or third-party vendors.

- **Isolated Use Cases**: AI efforts are isolated within specific departments (e.g., marketing using AI for customer segmentation) with little coordination across the business.

Focus Areas:

- Increase awareness of AI's potential.

- Begin building a basic understanding of AI technologies.

- Conduct pilot projects to test AI capabilities.

2. Managed (AI Experimentation & Exploration)

At the **Managed** stage, the organization begins to formalize its AI efforts. AI is no longer just experimental but is beginning to be integrated into specific business functions. The organization starts to recognize AI's potential for solving real business problems and starts to adopt AI solutions with a more structured approach. However, AI initiatives are still in their early stages and may not yet have a broad organizational impact.

Characteristics:

- **Defined AI Use Cases**: AI is being explored for specific use cases (e.g., chatbots for customer service, predictive analytics for sales forecasts).

- **Dedicated AI Team**: A dedicated team or individual is tasked with AI initiatives, though AI is still seen as a departmental or niche function rather than an enterprise-wide priority.

- **Data Strategy Development**: There is an emerging focus on improving data collection, management, and integration to feed AI models.

- **Early Adoption**: The organization begins to see some positive results, such as improved efficiencies or cost savings in specific areas.

Focus Areas:

- Develop a clear AI strategy and roadmap.

- Build a foundation for data collection and management.

- Identify key AI use cases across various departments.

- Begin to scale successful AI pilots.

3. Defined (AI Integration & Optimization)

At the **Defined** stage, AI is becoming more integrated into business processes. AI applications are now aligned with broader business goals, and there is a strategic focus on scaling AI throughout the organization.

The AI initiatives are no longer limited to one department or function, and the organization starts to realize the tangible business value of AI. AI is now seen as a core part of the organization's strategy and is making a meaningful impact on operations, customer experience, and decision-making.

Characteristics:

- **AI Across Functions**: AI is being implemented across multiple functions, including marketing, HR, finance, and operations.

- **Clear ROI and Business Impact**: The organization is beginning to measure the return on investment (ROI) of AI initiatives, and there is evidence of significant improvements in efficiency, decision-making, and customer satisfaction.

- **Data Infrastructure**: Strong data infrastructure is in place, and data is now treated as a strategic asset. Data scientists and engineers collaborate closely to ensure high-quality data is being fed into AI models.

- **Cross-functional Collaboration**: AI projects involve collaboration between different departments and functions, ensuring that AI aligns with organizational priorities.

Focus Areas:

- Scale AI across business functions.

- Align AI strategy with overall business goals.

- Strengthen data infrastructure and analytics capabilities.

- Develop governance frameworks for AI projects.

4. Managed (AI-Driven Decision Making & Predictive Insights)

At the **Managed** stage, AI is fully integrated into business operations, with organizations leveraging advanced AI techniques like predictive analytics, deep learning, and natural language processing (NLP) to drive decision-making.

AI is not just a tool but a core component of the decision-making process across the business. Organizations at this stage use AI for forecasting, automation, and deriving deep insights from vast amounts of data.

Characteristics:

- **AI-Powered Decision Making**: AI systems are making real-time recommendations or decisions in areas like customer service, inventory management, and financial planning.

- **Predictive Insights**: AI models are providing predictive insights that help organizations proactively address challenges, anticipate customer behavior, and identify new opportunities.

- **Automated Operations**: Many operational processes are automated through AI, reducing manual intervention and driving efficiency across the business.

- **Continuous Monitoring and Optimization**: AI systems are constantly monitored and optimized based on new data and business requirements.

Focus Areas:

- Leverage AI for predictive analytics and forecasting.

- Focus on automating complex processes.

- Enhance AI's role in real-time decision-making.

- Refine AI systems to continually optimize performance.

5. Optimized (AI at Scale & Innovation)

At the **Optimized** stage, AI has matured into a critical, transformative capability within the organization. AI is now driving significant innovation, with the company using AI to introduce new products, services, and business models.

AI is embedded deeply into the company's culture, operations, and customer experience, offering continuous value and providing a sustainable competitive advantage. AI innovation becomes an ongoing priority as the organization looks for new ways to apply AI to all aspects of its operations and strategy.

Characteristics:

- **AI as a Competitive Differentiator**: The organization uses AI to create new business models, disrupt markets, and stay ahead of competitors.

- **End-to-End Automation**: Many aspects of the business, from supply chain management to customer support, are fully automated with AI, improving efficiency and reducing human error.

- **AI-Driven Innovation**: AI is a key enabler of innovation, with organizations using AI to create new products, services, and personalized experiences for customers.

- **Cultural Adoption**: AI is fully embedded in the organization's culture, with continuous collaboration across departments and a commitment to AI-driven solutions.

Focus Areas:

- Scale AI innovations across global markets.

- Create new AI-powered products or services.

- Foster a culture of continuous AI experimentation and innovation.

- Explore advanced AI technologies like autonomous systems and deep learning.

AI Use Case Evaluation Framework

The **AI Use Case Evaluation Framework** is designed to help organizations assess and prioritize potential AI initiatives based on their strategic alignment, feasibility, and potential impact. As AI adoption expands, businesses are often faced with numerous opportunities, each requiring careful evaluation to determine its viability and business value. The evaluation framework offers a systematic approach to identify high-priority AI use cases that align with the organization's goals, are technically feasible, and can provide measurable outcomes. The framework includes several key criteria that organizations should consider when evaluating potential AI projects.

1. Strategic Fit

Strategic Fit assesses how well a potential AI use case aligns with the organization's broader business goals and objectives. AI initiatives should not be pursued in isolation, but rather as part of the larger strategic vision. For a use case to be valuable, it must contribute directly to the organization's mission, vision, and growth strategy.

Key Considerations:

- **Alignment with Organizational Goals**: Does the AI use case support key business objectives such as increasing revenue, enhancing customer satisfaction, improving operational efficiency, or driving innovation?

- **Impact on Competitive Advantage**: How will the use case help the organization differentiate itself from competitors? Will it create a unique value proposition or enable the business to lead in a specific market?

- **Long-term Vision**: Does the use case contribute to the organization's long-term AI roadmap, or is it a short-term initiative? It's essential to ensure that the AI use case supports the future vision of the business.

Example:

For a company that is focused on improving customer experience, an AI use case involving personalized product recommendations would have a strong strategic fit. It directly supports the goal of enhancing customer engagement and retention.

2. Impact Potential

Impact Potential evaluates the expected value that a specific AI use case can bring to the organization in terms of business outcomes. This includes both direct benefits (e.g., increased revenue or cost savings) and indirect benefits (e.g., improved brand reputation or customer loyalty). A high-impact AI use case has the potential to drive significant business transformation and provide measurable outcomes.

Key Considerations:

- **Financial Value**: What are the potential financial benefits of implementing the AI solution? This could be in terms of increased sales, cost reduction, or improved operational efficiency.

- **Innovation and Differentiation**: Will the AI use case enable the company to innovate, create new products or services, or differentiate itself in the marketplace?

- **Customer and Employee Impact**: How will the AI use case impact the customer experience, satisfaction, and retention? What benefits will employees gain in terms of productivity, reduced manual work, or job enrichment?

Example:

An AI system designed to optimize supply chain operations and reduce inventory waste could have a significant impact potential by reducing operational costs and improving profitability while enhancing the overall customer experience through faster delivery times.

3. Technical Feasibility

Technical Feasibility assesses whether the organization has the necessary infrastructure, data, and technical capabilities to implement the AI use case successfully. It's essential to evaluate the availability of the data required for AI model training, the technical expertise within the organization, and the capability of existing infrastructure to support the AI solution.

Key Considerations:

- **Data Availability and Quality**: Is there enough high-quality data to train AI models effectively? Does the organization already have access to the required data sources, or would new data need to be collected?

- **Algorithmic and Technical Expertise**: Does the organization have the required knowledge and technical capabilities (e.g., AI expertise, machine learning algorithms, software development) to build and deploy the AI model?

- **Infrastructure Requirements**: Does the organization have the necessary infrastructure (e.g., cloud services, computational power, storage capacity) to support the AI system? Will the infrastructure need significant upgrades or investments?

Example:

For an AI-driven fraud detection system, technical feasibility would depend on the availability of transactional data, historical fraud data for model training, and the capacity to process and analyze large amounts of data in real-time.

4. Risk Assessment

Risk Assessment considers the potential risks associated with implementing the AI use case. These risks could be ethical, regulatory, operational, or technical in nature. It's important to anticipate and mitigate any risks that might arise from the AI implementation to avoid negative consequences, whether related to legal compliance, data privacy, or unintended operational disruptions.

Key Considerations:

- **Ethical Risks**: Could the AI use case lead to biased outcomes, discrimination, or unintended consequences? Is the AI solution designed to ensure fairness and transparency? Does it align with ethical guidelines and best practices for AI usage?

- **Regulatory Compliance**: Does the AI initiative comply with relevant laws, regulations, and industry standards (e.g., GDPR, data privacy laws, financial regulations)? Are there specific regulatory requirements that need to be addressed?

- **Operational Risks**: What are the operational risks of AI implementation? Could there be disruptions to business operations, particularly in critical areas like customer service or financial transactions?

- **Security Risks**: Is the AI system secure from potential cybersecurity threats, such as data breaches or adversarial attacks that could manipulate the model's output?

Example:

An AI-powered recruitment system could face ethical risks if it inadvertently introduces bias by favoring certain demographic groups over others. Ensuring fairness, transparency, and bias mitigation techniques are applied would be critical to address these risks.

5. Implementation Timeline and Resource Allocation

Beyond the key criteria, it's also important to consider the timeline and resource allocation for AI use case implementation. Understanding how long it will take to deploy the AI solution, the costs involved, and whether the necessary resources are available are all important aspects of successful implementation.

Key Considerations:

- **Time to Market**: How long will it take to implement the AI solution? What is the expected timeline for achieving initial results and scaling the solution?

- **Resource Commitment**: Are the necessary resources (personal, budget, tools) available to implement the use case? Will new resources be required, and if so, can they be secured within the organization's constraints?

Example:

An AI-based marketing automation tool that segments customers based on behavior patterns might take several months to develop, implement, and test, requiring resources for data collection, algorithm development, and user training.

6. Scalability and Sustainability

Finally, the scalability and sustainability of the AI solution are crucial factors in evaluating use cases. AI initiatives that are scalable can grow with the business, handling increasing data volumes, business complexity, or new business functions.

Additionally, the sustainability of AI solutions ensures that they remain effective over time, adaptable to evolving business needs, and cost-effective in the long term.

Key Considerations:

- **Scalability**: Will the AI solution be able to handle increased loads as the business grows or expands? Can it be adapted to new markets or business functions?

- **Long-term Maintenance**: What will the ongoing maintenance and support look like? Will the AI model need regular updates and improvements, and does the organization have the resources to support this overtime?

- **Sustainability**: Does the use case contribute to sustainable business practices, such as energy-efficient AI models or practices that support long-term growth and stability?

Example:

An AI-powered customer service chatbot may be initially deployed to handle a small volume of customer inquiries but needs to be scalable to manage millions of interactions during peak seasons, requiring robust infrastructure and ongoing model improvements.

AI Readiness Assessment

The **AI Readiness Assessment** is a comprehensive tool or questionnaire designed to evaluate an organization's preparedness for adopting and implementing artificial intelligence (AI) solutions. It helps identify gaps and opportunities in key areas such as leadership commitment, talent and skills, data infrastructure, and organizational culture.

By conducting a thorough AI readiness assessment, organizations can determine whether they are equipped to successfully deploy AI and scale it over time, or if they need to invest in specific areas to enhance their readiness for AI adoption. This evaluation allows companies to make informed decisions and take proactive steps to ensure the smooth and successful integration of AI technologies into their operations.

1. Leadership Commitment

Leadership Commitment is one of the most critical factors influencing the success of AI adoption in an organization. Without strong buy-in from top executives and a clear vision from leadership, AI initiatives are likely to falter. Leaders must not only endorse the use of AI but also actively support and champion AI initiatives within the organization.

A lack of commitment at the leadership level can result in insufficient resources, fragmented efforts, or a lack of alignment with the organization's strategic goals.

Key Questions to Assess Leadership Commitment:

- **Is there a clear AI vision articulated by the leadership team?** Do the top executives understand the value and potential of AI in driving business transformation and innovation?

- **Do executives actively advocate for AI adoption?** Are leaders encouraging the integration of AI across different departments, and are they investing in AI-related projects?

- **Is AI a strategic priority for the organization?** Are AI initiatives aligned with the long-term business goals, and are executives setting measurable objectives for AI success?

- **Do leaders understand the broader implications of AI?** Is there a recognition of the ethical, regulatory, and operational considerations involved in AI adoption?

Example:

In a manufacturing company, the CEO may need to demonstrate leadership commitment by not only endorsing AI projects for predictive maintenance but also by championing cross-functional collaboration to integrate AI into the organization's operations and securing the necessary budget.

2. Talent and Skills

AI adoption requires specialized talent, including data scientists, AI researchers, machine learning engineers, and other technical experts, as well as business professionals who understand how to integrate AI into specific use cases. Assessing an organization's current talent pool is essential to determine whether the necessary skills are in place or if there are gaps that need to be addressed.

Key Questions to Assess Talent and Skills:

- **Do you have in-house AI expertise?**: Does the organization employ AI professionals who are capable of developing and deploying AI models and solutions?

- **Are your employees trained in the necessary skills for AI adoption?** Do employees have the foundational knowledge of AI, machine learning, data analytics, and relevant programming languages?

- **Do you have cross-functional collaboration between technical and business teams?** Is there a culture of collaboration between AI specialists and business units to ensure AI initiatives address real business challenges?

- **Are there opportunities for upskilling and reskilling?** Does the organization invest in developing AI skills within the workforce, either through training programs or partnerships with educational institutions?

Example:

A retail company may recognize the need to hire data scientists and machine learning engineers to develop an AI-driven recommendation engine, while also offering training to its marketing team to better understand and utilize AI-driven insights.

3. Data and Infrastructure

AI systems rely heavily on data to function. An organization's ability to collect, store, manage, and analyze large volumes of high-quality data directly impacts the success of AI initiatives. Having the right **data infrastructure** in place is a fundamental requirement for AI adoption. This includes access to clean, well-organized data, robust data pipelines, and scalable storage and computing resources.

Key Questions to Assess Data and Infrastructure:

- **Do you have access to high-quality, relevant data?** Is the organization collecting the necessary data for AI applications, and is it structured or processed in a way that allows for effective analysis?

- **Is your data centralized and easily accessible?** Are data silos present across departments, or is there a unified data strategy that allows for seamless data sharing and access across the organization?

- **Do you have the computational power needed for AI?** Does the organization have the necessary cloud or on-premises infrastructure to support the computing demands of AI models, including access to GPUs or specialized hardware?

- **Are data privacy and security measures in place?**: Does the organization adhere to data privacy regulations and best practices to ensure sensitive data is protected and used responsibly?

Example:

A healthcare organization looking to implement AI for predictive analytics in patient care needs to ensure that it has access to a centralized patient data repository, equipped with structured data from electronic health records (EHR), and the infrastructure to process large datasets in real time.

4. Culture and Governance

An organization's **culture and governance** framework plays a pivotal role in ensuring responsible, effective AI adoption. AI initiatives require a culture of innovation and collaboration, where stakeholders across the business understand the value of AI and are motivated to contribute to its success. At the same time, organizations must establish clear **governance** structures to manage AI projects, mitigate risks, and ensure ethical AI usage.

Key Questions to Assess Culture and Governance:

- **Is there a culture of innovation within the organization?** Does the company encourage experimentation, knowledge sharing, and continuous learning, especially regarding emerging technologies like AI?

- **Do employees at all levels understand AI and its potential?** Is there an awareness and understanding of AI across different teams, from executives to operational staff, and is AI seen as a tool to improve business processes rather than a threat?

- **Do you have clear AI governance and ethical guidelines?** Are there established frameworks to ensure AI projects are implemented responsibly, with attention to bias mitigation, fairness, and transparency?

- **Is there an oversight mechanism in place?** Does the organization have a dedicated AI governance body or team to oversee AI projects, ensuring compliance with laws and regulations, and monitoring the long-term impact of AI?

Example:

A financial services company may build a governance framework for its AI-driven credit scoring system, ensuring that data usage is ethical, models are transparent, and there are regular audits to avoid discriminatory practices.

5. Risk Management and Ethical Considerations

AI initiatives inherently involve risks related to data privacy, security, and ethical implications such as bias or discrimination.

Organizations need to assess how well they are equipped to identify and manage these risks, ensuring that AI systems are used responsibly and in compliance with legal and regulatory standards.

Key Questions to Assess Risk Management:

- **Do you have an ethical AI framework in place?** Does the organization have policies to ensure fairness, transparency, and accountability in AI systems, and do they address issues like bias, discrimination, and accountability?

- **Are risks associated with data usage and AI models actively monitored?** Does the organization have a process for identifying, evaluating, and mitigating risks such as data breaches, model errors, or regulatory non-compliance?

Example:

In a recruitment AI system, the company must ensure that the algorithms are tested for fairness and are not inadvertently reinforcing biases based on gender, race, or age, and that any discriminatory outcomes are addressed promptly.

AI Risk Management Framework

The **AI Risk Management Framework** is a comprehensive tool designed to assess, mitigate, and manage the various risks associated with AI implementation. Given the significant potential for AI to transform industries, it is critical that organizations adopt a proactive approach to identify and address potential risks, particularly in areas related to ethics, privacy, security, and compliance.

The risks associated with AI technologies—ranging from biased decision-making to data breaches and regulatory non-compliance—can have profound implications on an organization's reputation, legal standing, and operational integrity. Therefore, the AI Risk Management Framework helps ensure that AI solutions are deployed responsibly and ethically while maintaining stakeholder trust.

This framework addresses key risk areas that must be carefully managed during the lifecycle of AI projects, such as **bias and fairness**, **data privacy and security**, and **transparency and explainability**. By systematically evaluating and mitigating these risks, organizations can foster responsible AI use, ensuring that the technology's benefits are maximized while minimizing potential harm.

1. Bias and Fairness Assessment

AI models are built using large datasets, and these datasets can often reflect historical biases or systemic inequalities present in society. A **Bias and Fairness Assessment** is essential to ensure that AI models do not perpetuate or amplify biases that could result in unfair or discriminatory outcomes, whether in hiring, lending, law enforcement, or other applications. This risk is particularly important in high-stakes AI use cases, where biased decisions can lead to legal repercussions, loss of trust, or ethical violations.

Key Elements of Bias and Fairness Assessment:

- **Bias Detection**: Identifying whether AI models show any bias in predictions, recommendations, or decisions based on sensitive attributes such as race, gender, age, or socioeconomic status.

    - *Example*: An AI hiring tool might unintentionally favor male candidates over female candidates if trained on historical hiring data where gender imbalance exists.

- **Fairness Evaluation**: Ensuring that AI models treat all demographic groups equitably and that decisions do not disproportionately disadvantage certain groups.

- *Example*: A credit scoring model that penalizes certain communities unfairly due to biased training data, which could impact people from specific ethnic backgrounds or lower-income areas.

- **Bias Mitigation Strategies**: Implementing techniques to mitigate bias in AI systems, such as data preprocessing to remove biased features, algorithmic adjustments, and ongoing model monitoring.

  - *Example*: Rebalancing the dataset to ensure equal representation of different groups or using fairness-aware algorithms that penalize biased predictions.

Assessment Process:

- **Model Audits**: Conduct regular audits to evaluate the fairness of AI systems, using statistical measures like disparity analysis or equalized odds to detect biases.

- **Bias Correction**: If biases are detected, adopt techniques such as reweighting, re-sampling, or adversarial debiasing to address and minimize the impact of unfair outcomes.

- **Stakeholder Input**: Engage with diverse stakeholders, including domain experts and affected communities, to understand potential biases and ensure fairness across the system.

2. Data Privacy and Security

AI systems rely heavily on large datasets, many of which contain sensitive and personal information. **Data Privacy and Security** risks are therefore paramount.

Organizations must ensure that AI systems comply with privacy regulations such as the **General Data Protection Regulation (GDPR)** and maintain robust data security practices to protect user data from breaches or unauthorized access.

Mishandling of data can lead to severe legal consequences, loss of customer trust, and reputational damage.

Key Elements of Data Privacy and Security:

- **Data Collection and Consent**: Ensuring that data used in AI models is obtained with proper consent, and that users are informed about how their data will be used.

○ *Example*: A healthcare AI application that requires patient consent to use medical records for analysis, ensuring that patients understand how their data will contribute to AI-powered diagnostics.

- **Data Encryption and Anonymization**: Applying encryption techniques to protect sensitive data during storage and transmission, as well as anonymizing personally identifiable information (PII) to reduce privacy risks.

    ○ *Example*: Encrypting patient data in a medical AI system so that unauthorized parties cannot access personal health information.

- **Compliance with Regulations**: Adhering to data protection laws, such as GDPR, HIPAA, or the California Consumer Privacy Act (CCPA), ensuring that AI systems meet legal standards regarding data storage, processing, and user rights.

    ○ *Example*: Implementing GDPR-compliant features like the right to access, correct, or delete personal data and ensuring that AI systems handle such requests in a timely manner.

- **Data Retention and Deletion**: Implementing policies for data retention, ensuring that personal data is only kept as long as necessary and is securely deleted once no longer needed for AI applications.

Assessment Process:

- **Privacy Impact Assessments (PIAs)**: Conduct PIAs to evaluate the potential risks to user privacy when deploying AI systems and to identify measures to mitigate those risks.

- **Security Testing**: Regularly test AI systems for vulnerabilities, using techniques like penetration testing and vulnerability scans, to ensure that data is protected from unauthorized access.

- **Compliance Audits**: Periodically review AI systems for compliance with relevant data privacy laws and regulatory standards, adjusting protocols as necessary.

3. Transparency and Explainability

One of the primary concerns surrounding AI systems, especially in decision-making processes, is their **transparency** and **explainability**. Stakeholders—including users, regulatory bodies, and even developers—must be able to understand how AI models arrive at their decisions. Lack of transparency can lead to mistrust, particularly when decisions have significant consequences, such as in hiring, lending, or healthcare applications. **Explainability** is essential for building stakeholder trust and ensuring accountability in AI decisions.

Key Elements of Transparency and Explainability:

- **Model Interpretability**: Assessing whether AI models can be interpreted and explained in a way that makes sense to human stakeholders, especially non-technical users.

  - *Example*: A loan approval AI system should provide explanations for why certain applicants were approved or rejected, detailing factors like credit score, income, and debt levels.

- **Post-Hoc Explanation Techniques**: Using techniques like LIME (Local Interpretable Model-Agnostic Explanations) or SHAP (Shapley Additive Explanations) to generate understandable explanations for model decisions, even if the model itself is complex (e.g., deep learning).

○ *Example*: A recommendation algorithm can use SHAP values to explain why a particular product was recommended to a user, allowing users to see which factors (e.g., past behavior, preferences) influenced the decision.

- **Model Audits for Transparency**: Implementing processes to audit and assess AI models regularly to ensure they provide clear, understandable justifications for their decisions.

  ○ *Example*: Conducting regular transparency reviews of predictive policing AI systems to ensure they are making fair and explainable predictions that stakeholders can trust.

Assessment Process:

- **Explainability Testing**: Evaluate AI models for their ability to produce understandable outputs. In complex systems, ensure that interpretable models or explanation tools are integrated into the system for transparency.

- **Stakeholder Engagement**: Involve users, regulatory bodies, and external experts in the evaluation of model decisions, providing them with explanations and rationales for how the AI system works.

- **Documentation of Decisions**: Keep comprehensive documentation of the AI model development process, including the rationale behind decisions made during model selection, data preparation, and algorithm choices.

4. AI Governance and Ethical Considerations

In addition to technical risk factors, AI adoption also carries ethical implications. **AI Governance and Ethical Considerations** are essential for ensuring that AI systems are deployed responsibly and that their use aligns with ethical principles. Establishing strong governance frameworks, clear policies, and a commitment to ethical AI principles can help organizations mitigate the risks of unethical practices and potential harm from AI technologies.

Key Elements of AI Governance:

- **Ethical AI Framework**: Developing a set of ethical guidelines to govern AI usage within the organization, ensuring fairness, accountability, and transparency.

- **Stakeholder Oversight**: Implementing governance structures like AI ethics boards or advisory panels that include diverse stakeholders to oversee AI projects and ensure they meet ethical standards.

- **Continuous Monitoring and Accountability**: Creating systems to continuously monitor AI systems' impact, providing mechanisms for accountability when AI decisions have negative consequences.

Assessment Process:

- **Ethical Audits**: Conduct regular audits to evaluate the ethical implications of AI models, identifying any potential harms, conflicts, or unintended consequences.

- **Ethics Training**: Provide training to employees involved in AI projects on ethical principles, ensuring they understand the importance of bias mitigation, transparency, and fairness in AI development.

Final Chapter: Towards a Future Powered by Generative AI

As we conclude this exploration of the fascinating world of **Generative Artificial Intelligence**, we've delved into its diverse applications, the challenges it presents, best practices for implementation, and the strategies necessary to maximize its impact. Throughout this book, we've seen how generative AI is not just a powerful tool, but a technology that redefines the boundaries of what's possible in business and beyond. From enhancing operational efficiency to creating new customer experiences, to innovating products and services, generative AI stands as a pivotal element in the digital transformation of any organization.

It is crucial to remember that adopting generative AI is not an isolated or immediate process, but a journey that requires reflection, planning, and adaptation. Organizations that can skillfully understand and manage the technical, ethical, and strategic aspects of this technology will be the ones that shape the future.

The world of generative AI is still evolving, and while its potential is vast, so are the challenges. This is why continued learning, feedback, and a commitment to ethical standards are necessary to ensure that AI works in harmony with human goals, values, and needs. It's a collective effort that involves leadership, teams, customers, and society at large.

As you move forward, whether you are a leader, practitioner, or stakeholder in AI adoption, I encourage you to keep an open mind, embrace change, and remain agile in the face of ongoing technological evolution. By doing so, you not only unlock immense value for your organization but also contribute to the responsible and innovative development of AI for the betterment of society.

Thank you for taking this journey with me. I hope the insights shared throughout this book help guide your organization towards a successful, impactful, and sustainable AI-driven future.

THANK YOU FOR READING!

Thank you for dedicating your time to reading this book. It has been my privilege to share insights, strategies, and practical advice to help you navigate the transformative potential of Generative AI. My hope is that this book has provided you with valuable tools, sparked new ideas, and empowered you to take meaningful steps toward innovation and growth in your business or personal endeavors.

If you found this book useful, engaging, or thought-provoking, I would be incredibly grateful if you could take a few moments to leave a positive review where you purchased it. Your feedback not only helps others discover this resource but also motivates me to continue writing and refining future works to better serve readers like you.

Reviews are a powerful way to connect with others who might benefit from these ideas, and your voice can make a real difference in spreading knowledge and inspiration. Thank you for your support, and I wish you every success on your journey!

With gratitude,

Ethan Westwood

SMART B O O K S

www.ingramcontent.com/pod-product-compliance
Lightning Source LLC
LaVergne TN
LVHW022337060326
832902LV00022B/4086